14.60

BIBLIOTECA DI BIBLIOGRAFIA ITALIANA
LXXXIX

BONNER MITCHELL

ITALIAN CIVIC PAGEANTRY
IN THE
HIGH RENAISSANCE

A DESCRIPTIVE BIBLIOGRAPHY
OF TRIUMPHAL ENTRIES AND SELECTED
OTHER FESTIVALS FOR STATE OCCASIONS

FIRENZE
LEO S. OLSCHKI EDITORE
MCMLXXIX

ISBN 88 222 2841 3

PREFACE

In recent decades scholars from a number of different disciplines have become increasingly interested in the very rich material of cultural history to be found in the records of civic celebrations or « festivals » (*feste, fêtes, Feiern*) of past centuries.

There is now a considerable body of scholarship, and festival students have also come together on several occasions – most notably those in France resulting in Jean Jacquot's three volumes of *Les Fêtes de la Renaissance* – to read papers and exchange ideas. Nevertheless the field cannot be said to be a well-established one, for it lacks both permanent organizations and specialized journals. One result of the primitive state of organization is a scarcity of bibliographies. Except when he is interested in an occasion that has already received a good, systematic modern study – still a rarity – a festival scholar often has no bibliography to take as his point of departure. There are, to be sure, some important bibliographical contributions. Thus John Landwehr has prepared a bibliography of printed sources for *Splendid Ceremonies: State Entries and Royal Funerals in the Low Countries, 1515-1791* (Nieuwkoop, B. De Graaf; Leiden, A. W. Sijthoff 1971). In Italy there are now some very valuable compilations dealing with celebrations in particular cities, usually for periods later than the one with which we are concerned here. For Florence, Giovanna Gaeta Bertalà and Annamaria Petrioli Tofani have prepared a fine catalogue of *Feste e apparati medicei da Cosimo I a Cosimo II* (Firenze, Olschki 1969). For Rome there has appeared the first volume of M. Fagiolo Dell'Arco and S. Carandini's *L'effimero barocco: struttura delle feste della Roma del Seicento* (Roma, Bulzoni 1977). For Naples there is Franco Mancini's *Feste ed apparati civili e religiosi in Napoli dal viceregno alla capitale* (Napoli, Edizioni Scientifiche Italiane 1968). Regarding Italy in our own period, there is a great deal of pertinent material in the careful, far-ranging bibliography of festivals in the reign of Charles V appended by Jean Jacquot to his fundamental essay *Panorama des fêtes et cérémonies du règne* (included in the list of studies concerning several festivals at the end of this volume). This bibliography is, however, very properly, focused on one prince and his son. There exist, to my knowledge, no annual or other serial bibliographies devoted especially to festival studies, although Anne-Marie Lecoq's essay on the state of the field *La* Città Festeggiante: *les fêtes publiques au XVe et XVIe siècles* («La Revue de l'Art», no. 33, 1976, pp. 83-100) contains much detailed information on recent bibliography. There are of course serial bibliographies for various larger fields – history, art history, musicology, and literary studies – that include festival studies, but the references are scattered and hard to find. The organization of a group of scholars to prepare an annual specialized bibliography would be a major step forward for the field.

The Italian festivals for the historical period covered by the present bibliography have also been less well studied than those of later periods, notably those of the immediately following second halt of the sixteenth century, and the relative lack of modern studies increases the difficulty of finding references to sources. The reason the period has been less studied is an understandable one: the comparative scarcity of surviving graphic material. A festival is clearly more interesting if there are drawings of the *apparati*, not only for art historians but also for historians from other disciplines. When, however, good written descriptions have come down, as for many festivals of the period, there is still rich documentation for the history of form and style. Less strictly literary material has survived as well, though in a few cases, most remarkably the Campidoglio celebrations of 1513 and the marriage of Cosimo I in 1539, we have a wealth of occasional verses. Even here, however, descriptive accounts are very helpful, as when an observer gives the gist of recited verses or interprets an allegorical dramatic skit. Moreover, in one very important class of surviving literary material, Latin inscriptions from *apparati*, the period is almost as rich as those that follow. The scarcity of surviving music – that of 1539 being apparently the only identifiable corpus – is more frustrating. At most the chroniclers may tell us what instruments were used or, very rarely, mention the name of musicians; usually – most tantalizingly in the case of the meeting between Leo X and Francis I in Bologna – they simply praise the beauty of the music.

The importance of the period for the history of state pageantry, as well as for cultural history generally, is evident. It includes the ill-defined moment known as the High Renaissance, and in civic festivals, as in so many other domains, it sees the triumph of conscious classical revival, a movement that soon spreads from Italy to other European countries. In political history it coincides almost precisely with the dynamic period of the « Italian Wars », that of the foreign invasions and of the destruction of most Italian aspirations toward political liberty. The coverage of this bibliography begins by design in 1494 with the receptions of King Charles VIII of France, come to conquer the kingdom of Naples. At its end the French have been virtually driven from Italy and Spanish-Imperial domination, more or less direct, is evident almost everywhere. The majority of the grand entries of the period come during the intimidating tours of foreign sovereigns. After the expedition of Charles VIII in 1494-95, there were those of Louis XII to northern Italy between 1499 and 1509, and that of Francis I in 1515. (Francis' second expedition in 1525 ended in disaster before he could be received in major cities). Charles V, the most imposing Holy Roman Emperor since Charlemagne, and the most interested in Italian affairs since Frederick II, came to the peninsula many times, with grand triumphal entries in 1529-30, 1532, 1535-36, and 1541. His son Prince Phillip, soon to be king of Spain, crossed the country from Genoa to the borders of the Empire, with magnificent receptions along the way, in 1548-49. In scanning this bibliography of civic occasions, one can glimpse the pattern of great cities' unhappy political fortunes. Milan (who, it is true, had not been much more fortunate with its own duke Ludovico il Moro) receives conquering French kings in the early part of the century and later welcomes Charles V and his son Phillip as virtual masters. Naples is briefly conquered by Charles VIII at the beginning of the period and later welcomes Ferdinand of Aragon and Charles V as its foreign sovereigns. Rome, after submitting to the unwelcome visit of Charles

VIII in 1494-95, in 1536 greets Charles V, whose troops had sacked it nine years before, as someone a great deal more redoubtable than an obedient Christian prince. Genoa, after receiving Louis XII as its master – willingly in 1502 and with terror in 1507 – clings to a formal remnant of independence as its chief citizen Andrea Doria presides over the receptions of Charles V and Prince Phillip in later decades. Florence, with a newly restored republican regime, barely manages to hold its dignity in the unwelcome visit of Charles VIII, but by the 1530's its Duke Alessandro receives Charles V as a vassal receives his lord, and the planners of the festivities for the marriage of Cosimo I insert into the *apparati* and poetic compositions numerous obsequious allusions to the emperor. Only Venice, despite a bad scare at the time of the League of Cambrai, remains for the most part serenely independent. It receives none of the foreign conquerors of Italy during our period, flattering only its allies with aquatic entries on the Bucentaur and with ummatched princely entertainments.

Italy had still in the sixteenth century a remarkable variety of governmental forms – the papacy, the kingdom of Naples, republics, and many sorts of principalities – and all of them had their own traditions of civic pageantry that were evident not only on domestic occasions but also in the reception of foreign visitors. Thus in Naples Charles V was received by his own viceroy and by the city's five *seggi*, in Rome by the pope and cardinals and by the formal remnant of the S.P.Q.R., or republican city government, in Florence and Mantua by native princes who were also vassals, and in Lucca by a genuine republic that did not wish to acknowledge any allegiance to the Empire. The variety of civic pageantry was thus much greater in Italy than in such relatively well-knit kingdoms as France and England.

The word « festival », with its relatively recent currency among historical scholars, has a rather broad meaning. This bibliography does not aim, of course, to deal with all Italian festive occasions of the period, and even though the title includes some restrictions, it remains for me to make clear what kinds of festivals, or *feste*, I have tried to include. I have, first, been concerned only with civic festivals and pageantry and have thus excluded the primarily folkloric or popular, the primarily sportive, and the primarily religious. This distinction cannot, however, be absolute. The mass of the populace participated, at least as spectators, in the triumphal entries of sovereigns, though these were planned by learned men. There were sporting events, often chivalric ones such as jousts, for state visits. There were religious elements not only in coronations and investitures but also in grand entries, when the entering prince was nearly always greeted by prelates as well as by civic officials, and when he nearly always stopped at the Duomo on his way to the palace designated for his residence. And in the case of Rome and the States of the Church, nearly all state occasions were ecclesiastical ones as well. In the triumphal return of Pope Julius II in 1507, secular and religious motifs are quite inextricably tangled in the artistic and dramatic presentations. In Venice it was customary to invoke Saint Mark on virtually all state occasions, and many civic ceremonies were held on the steps of his basilica. Nevertheless, I have tried to make the predominantly civic character of a celebration the first criterion of selections.

The second criterion has been that of the occasional and topical quality of the civic festivals chosen: investitures, dynastic marriages, « summit conferences », and, above all, triumphal entries. There were, of course, civic celebrations that were annual: most notably the observances of religious holidays associated with patron saints, such as that of Saint John the Baptist in Florence and that of the Assumption of the Virgin Mary in Sienna. In Venice, as we learn from Giustina Renier-Michiel's charming book of a century and a half ago *Origine delle feste veneziane* (Milano, Editori degli Annali Universali delle Scienze e dell'Industria 1829, 6 vols. in 2), the number of annual celebrations of patriotic inspiration was really astonishing. In some cities, particularly Rome, the *apparati* for carnival could have civic and political themes. I could not undertake to deal with all the annual celebrations for a period of over half a century, although I have included one Florentine San Giovanni, that of 1545, one Florentine carnival, that of 1513, and one Roman carnival, that of 1513, because they did have important civic motifs in their artistic presentations, and also so that they might serve as examples of their genres.

I have been influenced in my choices also by the importance of artistic and literary creations inspired by various occasions. Sometimes the visit of a sovereign, whether because of hastiness or of political circumstances, did not entail the construction of special *apparati* or other elaborate preparations. I have generally left out such occasions, examples being an entry of Louis XII into Milan in 1502 and most of the entries of Charles VIII during his return journey from Naples to France. I have, however, felt obliged to include a few unelaborate entries, such as that of Charles VIII into Rome on the last day of 1494, because of their dramatic quality and their great political significance.

I have also been dependent on the availability of printed documentation, and there have been several state occasions of potential interest about which I have not been able to learn enough to justify including them. Examples are the visit of Charles V to Palermo in 1535 and that of King Henry II to Turin in 1548, at the beginning of his reign. Perhaps future scholars will be able to fill some of these *lacunae*.

The coverage may seem at first glance to be willfully partial. While I have a considerable amount of material for Rome, Florence, and Milan, there is markedly less for other important cities, and for a few very little or, indeed, none. Thus Ferrara, a center of courtly entertainments extremely important in theatrical history, has only three civic occasions listed. Naples, one of the largest Italian cities, has only four. Turin, now a city of the first rank and then already the seat of a duchy, though quite small, has only one. Many cities of importance, such as Modena, Verona, and Urbino, with its famous cultured court, have none. The reasons for this apparent imbalance lie in the political history of the period, in the outcome of battles, and in the projects of triumphal tours and summit meetings. I have not provided a balanced survey of the festive activities in particular cities – even, perhaps, of their civic celebrations, if one considers the annual events – but have tried to include the grandest and most culturally interesting state occasions in the country as a whole.

The study of civic festivals is, of course, a part of the larger field of theatrical history, and sometimes it overlaps with the more restricted one of the history of literary theatre. I have included some dozen occasions that entailed performances of literary comedies, classical Latin or in the new vernacular genre of the *commedia erudita*. It should not be supposed, however, that my survey presents an inclusive, or even a representative, picture of such performances, the majority of which took place during carnival, as part of a type of entertainments that I have not usually included. (The frequency of comedy performances would alone be sufficient to make a future special bibliography of Italian sixteenth-century carnival entertainments extremely useful). I cite editions of comedies played for state occasions only when the title of the edition refers to the occasion. Information about first editions may, however, be found in the fine bibliography of Achille Mango, which is consistently cited.

I hope that the summaries of individual festivals provided at the beginning of bibliographical lists may, taken together, permit an uninitiated reader to gain a basic picture of the civic pageantry of the period. These summaries are, however, nothing like comprehensive analyses. While in the cases of some simple or poorly known occasions I may have come near mentioning all the important elements of a festival, in those of the grander and better documented occasions, such as the main entries of Charles V, I am very far from having done so. The principal aim of these summaries is to provide scholars with enough information to allow them to decide whether they wish to look further into a particular festival.

The references are divided into sources and studies. This distinction has sometimes been tenuous, as in the cases of contemporary writers who were not witnesses and, also, in those of modern scholars who are publishing source material. In general I have listed all sixteenth-century references as sources, on the grounds that their authors may have had at least close second-hand reports or may have used written sources not now available. In the case of modern, or at least post-1600, publications of sixteenth-century material, I have simply tried to judge whether the publication was important mainly for its source material or for its interpretation and analysis. Scholars seeking first-hand information are therefore cautioned to consult the list of studies as well as that of sources.

My criteria for deciding whether a source or study was important enough to be included have been flexible, though not, I trust, incoherent. For poorly known festivals I have listed short references that might have been left out for better known occasions. A few basic sources such as Vandenesse's journal of the travels of Charles V and a few monumental studies such as Pastor's history of the papacy have been cited even when they contain little information.

Among the studies listed, focused monographs and essays form only a minority. Most references are to subsidiary accounts of festivals in books and essays on larger subjects. In these very numerous cases, my references are to exact pages of relevant passages rather than to the work as a whole. Recent studies are also in a minority. A very large proportion of studies are from the nineteenth century, many of them either the very specialized publications that Italians used to print at their own expense for the *nozze* of friends, or articles in the many journals of local societies, whose vast wealth of often poorly indexed historical material I fear I have not completely mined.

Among the sources, actual « festival books », or « livrets » in the term of French scholars, are much less numerous for our period than for the following ones. I have, however, found considerably more of them than I expected to. Surviving Cinquecento editions are very rare. I have listed the libraries, usually Italian, where I have consulted them, with the call number or *collocazione*. Sometimes, for the very important ones, I have also indicated whether they can be found in the British Museum, London, or the Bibliothèque Nationale, Paris, as well as in Italy. I have not shown American locations because the new *National Union Catalog* for pre-1956 imprints makes searching for them very easy.

Some of the older studies and scholarly editions, notably those published for *nozze*, are also hard to find, particularly outside of Italy, and that makes the preparation of new editions and new general studies in the field all the more desirable.

In the case of well-known works by foreign authors that have received Italian translations, I have nearly always chosen to cite the translation rather then the text in the original language. This is partly because most of the users of this bibliography will probably be Italian and partly because the Italian editions of several famous works, for example, Roscoe's *Life of Leo X* and Pastor's *History of the Popes*, have scholarly commentary and documents that do not exist in the original editions. For works that have had a number of editions, I have tried to choose the standard one, or at least a good recent one. I trust that readers will not have excessive difficulty in transferring my references from one edition to another.

The most serious weakness of this bibliography, a serious one indeed, is certainly the lack of references to manuscript sources. Locating and examining all these, in many different cities, would have meant years more of research and was impractical for this project. In numerous cases, however, the studies I list have cited manuscript material. I have indicated the presence of such references so that readers may find them and be led to the manuscripts themselves.

I have read all the items listed in the bibliography except the relatively few marked « not seen ». I have had the unpleasant experience of discovering after settling in Italy some things that are not available here but that I might have seen easily while working in the United States, England, or France earlier.

The almost fortuitous way in which I discovered some of my references makes it quite impossible for me to imagine that I have found all the important sources and studies. I can only hope, following earlier authors in this series, that for a time this bibliography will be the first place where students of its subject matter will look.

Among the abbreviations I have used, relatively few, I think only the following may require explanation:

N.p.   = place of publication not indicated.

N.d.   = date of publication not indicated.

N.pub. = publisher not indicated.

Cc.   = from the Italian « carte », meaning leaves as opposed to pages. Unless I have indicated the contrary, the leaves are unnumbered except within their signatures.

Sigs.   = signatures, or gatherings.

I am very grateful for the courtesy of the staffs of a number of libraries: the Ellis Library of my own University of Missouri-

Columbia; the libraries of the Warburg Institute and the British Museum, London; the Bibliothèque de l'Arsenal and the Bibliothèque Nationale, Paris; the Biblioteca Statale, Lucca; the Biblioteca Nazionale Braidense, Milan; the Biblioteca Apostolica Vaticana and the Biblioteca Nazionale Centrale Vittorio Emmanuele, Rome; the Biblioteca Riccardiana, the Biblioteca Marucelliana, and, above all, the Biblioteca Nazionale Centrale and the library of the Kuntshistorisches Institut, Florence. I wish to thank Miss Eve Borsook at the Kunsthistorisches Institut in Florence for reading the Florentine chapter and offering valuable criticism, and Mlle Anne-Marie Lecoq, *assistante* at the Collège de France in Paris, for generously helping me with some bibliographical searching.

I am indebted to the Research Council of the Graduate School of the University of Missouri-Columbia for subsidizing my research with a Summer Research Fellowship and a travel grant, and for making a contribution toward the cost of this publication.

B. M.

Florence 1979

BOLOGNA

I

1506, November 11. Triumphal Entry of Pope Julius II after His Defeat of the Bentivoglio Faction and Recovery of the City for the Papal States.

The pope (who had slept just inside the walls the night before) entered in a very elaborate procession including cardinals, other prelates, and numerous city officials, progressing slowly to San Pietro and then to the Palazzo Communale, where he was to stay. The entry was a deliberate echo of ancient triumphs, with officials tossing specially minted coins to the crowds, and with thirteen triumphal arches along the route. Preparations were, however, made hastily, and the arches seem to have been uncomplicated, with simple iconographical content. Of the some half dozen inscriptions that are preserved, several praised the pope as liberator of the city, conqueror of tyrants, and restorer of peace, and another exalted Bologna's tradition of learning. The identity of the artists who worked on the *apparati* does not seem to be known.

Sources

1. ALBERTINI, FRANCESCO, *Opusculum de mirabilibus novae urbis Romae*, hereausgegeben von R. Schmarsow, Heilbronn, Henninger 1886, pp. XXI-XXII.

An obsequious account in a contemporary work addressed to Pope Julius himself. The author captures the atmosphere of the triumph but deliberately omits description of the *apparati* and quotation of inscriptions.

2. ANONYMOUS, *Ingressus S. Patris D. D. N. Papae Julii Secondi in civitati Bononiae*, published by an anonymous editor, without notes. « Archivio Storico Lombardo », serie 2ª, anno II, 1875, pp. 185-188.

A letter dealing with planning for the procession of the pope's entry.

3. BERNARDI, *Cronache forlivesi*, pp. 201-202.

A highly enthusiastic account apparently by a witness, with, however, few details.

4. CONTI DA FOLIGNO, SIGISMONDO DE', *Le storie de' suoi tempi dal 1475 al 1510*, ora per la prima volta pubblicate nel testo latino con versione italiana a fronte. Roma, no pub., 1883, pp. 358-362.

An interesting account by one of the pope's secretaries who rode near him in the entry. Much information on the procession, little on the *apparati*. Records one inscription.

5. GHIRARDACCI, CHERUBINO, *Della historia di Bologna, parte terza*, a cura di Albano Sorbelli. In MURATORI, *Rerum Italicarum Scriptores*, tomo XXXIII, parte III, pp. 354-356.

A careful list and description of the procession, with little on the *apparati*.

6. GRASSI, *Le due spedizioni militari di Giulio II*, pp. 85-96.

A very informative account by the pope's master of ceremonies, a Bolognese, who seems to have been in charge of all arrangements. Very much attention to the order of the procession, less to the *apparati*. Five inscriptions are recorded. States that thirty-one arches had been ordered but only thirteen built. The main source.

7. SANUDO, *Diarii*, vol. VI, cols. 491-493.

In summaries of letters from several Venetian representatives, some description of the entry, with the text of two inscriptions.

Studies

8. MUZZI, *Annali della città di Bologna*, vol. V, pp. 507-510.

A good summary of the occasion with some information on the procession and the *apparati*.

9. PASTOR, *Storia dei papi*, vol. III, pp. 717-719.

The best modern summary, based on a large number of printed and ms. sources.

10. RINALDI, *Annales ecclesiastici*, tomus XI, pp. 489-490 (documents XXX-XXXII).

A good account with long quotations from Grassi's diary.

11. RODOCANACHI, *Le Pontificat de Jules II*, pp. 74-75.

A short account with some description of the procession and *apparati*.

12. VIZANI, *Historie della sua patria*, pp. 463-465.

A good description of the procession with no attention to the *apparati*.

II

1515, December 8-18. ENTRIES AND SOJOURNS OF POPE LEO X AND
KING FRANCIS I OF FRANCE, WHO WERE MEETING, AFTER THE FRENCH
VICTORY AT MARIGNAN, FOR POLITICAL AND ECCLESIASTICAL DIS-
CUSSIONS.

A somewhat disappointing state occasion for students of civic
festivals. There were far fewer artistic and literary undertakings
than for the meeting of Pope Clement VII and the Emperor Charles
V fifteen years later, and much less information has survived. December 8: entry of Leo X, with a relatively hostile reception by the
Bolognese, by the Porta Maggiore, where he was met by clergy
and city officials, with procession by the Torre degli Asinelli to the
Duomo and the Palazzo Communale, where he was to stay. *Apparati*: several arches of whose iconographical content little is known,
and, on the façade of the house of a prominent merchant, a temporary balcony with the arms of the pope, the king, and Cardinal
Giulio de' Medici, several inscriptions, and a number of figures
about which little is known. The planning of many of the *apparati*
is said (by Bernardi, below) to have been done by a humanist
named Feriano di Ubaldino. December 11: entry of Francis I, with
a very warm reception by the Bolognese, by the Porta San Felice,
met by prelates, city officials, and his allies the Venetian ambassadors, to the Palazzo Communale, where that evening he was received by the pope. *Apparati*: several triumphal arches of which
rather little is known. One drawing seems to survive (see Frommel,
below). December 13: a pontifical mass in San Petronio with the
king serving the pope. December 15: departure of the king. December 18: departure of the pope.

2

Sources

1. BARRILLON, *Journal*, vol. I, pp. 165-174.

A rather detailed witness account of the king's entry and subsequent meetings with the pope. There are, however, only general remarks about the entry *apparati*.

2. BERNARDI, *Cronache forlivesi*, pp. 427-433.

Apparently by a witness, naïve but detailed accounts of the two entries with some description of the *apparati* and the recording of several inscriptions, either in the original Latin or in mixed Latin and Italian. Several constructions that must have been triumphal arches are referred to as « ponte ». A major source.

3. FLORANGE, *Mémoires*, tome I, pp. 209-212, reprinted partly in GODEFROY, *Le Céremonial françois*, tome I, p. 752.

A short witness account with few details.

4. GRASSI, *Il diario di Leon X*, pp. 26-28.

By the pope's master of ceremonies, a few passages about the Bologna meeting. The most informative ones, quoted by Pastor and Rinaldi, below, are, however, left out of this edition.

5. SANUDO, *Diarii*, vol. XXI, cols. 375-381, 383-384, and 391-393.

A considerable amount of information in quotations or summaries of letters sent to Venice, including one from the young humanist Paolo Giovio, who was accompanying the pope. One letter mentions triumphal chariots for the entry of Francis I.

Studies

6. FROMMEL, *Baldassare Peruzzi als Maler und Zeichner*, pp. 13 and 76 and plate xcii c.

Publishes from the « Siena Sketchbook » associated with Peruzzi (but not all of his hand) the drawing of an *apparato* with fleurs-de-lys that he thinks may represent one of the constructions erected for the entry of Francis I. Peruzzi himself had accompanied the pope to Bologna, but it seems unlikely he had time actually to work on any of the *apparati* himself.

7. MADELIN, LOUIS, *De conventu bononiensi*, Paris, Plon-Nourrit 1900, pp. 52 and 59-80.

In a Sorbonne thesis, written in Latin, the author gives a good account of the two entries and of the later ceremonies, using all the important sources. The rest of the volume is concerned mainly with the political and ecclesiastical negotiations of the pope and king.

8. Muzzi, *Annali della città di Bologna*, vol. VI, pp. 105-113.

A good summary of events with particular information on the ceremonies of the meetings.

9. Pastor, *Storia dei papi*, vol. IV, parte I, pp. 85-90.

A good account of events with quotations from ms. letters of Alessandro Gabbioneta (an envoy from Mantua), from Grassi's diary, and from other sources.

10. Rinaldi, *Annales ecclesiastici*, tomus XII, pp. 106-110.

A rather full account of the entries and ceremonies with long quotations from Grassi's diary.

11. Rodocanachi, *Le Pontificat de Léon X*, pp. 89-98.

A good summary of events with numerous references.

12. Roscoe, *Vita e pontificato di Leon X*, vol. V, pp. 142-155, and vol. VI, pp. 291-303.

A very good summary of the occasion with extended quotations from Grassi's diary and with the text of an oration by the French chancellor Duprat.

13. Vizani, *Historie della sua patria*, pp. 518-519.

A short account of the conference with very little information on the entries.

III

1529, October 24-1530, March 22. Entries and Sojourns of Pope Clement VII and the Emperor Charles V, with Two Coronations of the Emperor.

A long and brilliant festive occasion rich with ceremonial and artistic content. October 24: entry of Clement VII, by the Porta Maggiore, with procession to Santa Maria del Tempio, then to the cathedral of San Pietro for a *Te Deum*, then to the Palazzo Communale. Principale *apparati*: an arch before the Porta Maggiore with the arms of the pope and emperor, two doric arches before the Palazzo Scrappi with biblical scenes, notably the anointing of David by Samuel, and inscriptions; an arch in the Piazza Maggiore with statues of God the Father, Saint Peter, Saint Paul, Saint Petronius,

Saint Ambrose, Clement VII, and several Virtues, as well as paintings of biblical scenes and inscriptions. November 5: entry of Charles V by the Porta San Felice in full military array, with procession to San Petronio, where he was received by the pope in a temporary edifice representing the Sala dei Concistori in the Vatican. Principal *apparati*: an arch in front of the Porta San Felice showing, among other things, the triumphs of Neptune and Bacchus; on the gate, the papal and imperial arms with medallions or sculptures representing Julius Caesar, Augustus, Scipio Africanus and other figures of ancient Roman history, a Janus before his closed temple, Apollo and the Muses, with an inscription calling for further victories of the emperor over the infidels; along the route, two doric arches with effigies of Victory and Glory, and columns topped with statues of Emperors Constantine, Charlemagne, and Sigismundus and King Ferdinand the Catholic of Spain. February 22, 1530: coronation of Charles with the Iron Crown of Lombardy in a chapel of the Palazzo. Many interesting ceremonial details. February 24: coronation of Charles by the pope with the imperial crown in San Petronio, which had been decorated to resemble Saint Peter's in Rome. Elaborate and lengthy ceremonies. The pope and the emperor had passed from the palace to San Petronio over a raised walkway in view of the crowd. After the coronation, Clement and Charles rode under the same *baldacchino* to the church of San Domenico, meant to represent Saint John-in-Lateran in Rome, where the emperor carried out his new ceremonial duties as a deacon of that cathedral and also created some new knights. In the evening, a banquet at the Palazzo Communale, with a fountain of wine and a roasting steer for the crowd on the Piazza Maggiore. March 4 or 8: playing of Agostino Ricchi's comedy *I tre tiranni* in a room of the Palazzo Communale before the pope, the emperor, and Beatrice di Portogallo, duchess of Savoy. March 23: departure of Charles V. March 31: departure of Clement VII. Artists said to have worked on the *apparati*: Amico Aspertini, Alfonso Lombardi, and Giorgio Vasari. Probably participation as well of all the other artists in the city, a number of whom are listed by Giordani, below, in his *Cronaca*, pp. 16-17. Three series of engravings showing the processions are listed below.

Sources

1. ANONYMOUS, *La cavalcata dell'Imperator C. V. nel suo ingresso in Bologna.* Plates printed in Venice probably in 1529 or 1530. Copies in the British Museum, London, and in the Uffizi Gallery, Florence.

The original edition not seen. Reproduced in facsimile, however, in Maxwell, *The Entry of the Emperor,* below.

2. ANONYMOUS, *Il superbo apparato fatto in Bologna alla incoronatione della Cesarea Maiesta Carolo V. imperatore de christiani.* N.p., n.d., but doubtless 1530, 4°, cc. 2. British Museum, London: C. 33. h5.

A short account of the second coronation and of the following procession. The title page has a woodcut showing the emperor, the pope, a figure who seems to be the doge of Venice, and two unidentified figures, one of them wearing a crown. A woodcut on the last page shows a triumphal chariot drawn by griffins and carrying an angel who is blowing a trumpet and holding a crown. The account is interesting for its many mentions of persons present, with special attention to Venetian representatives. This small publication is listed, but had not been seen, by Giordani, below.

3. [GONZAGA, LUIGI], *Cronaca del soggiorno di Carlo V in Italia,* pp. 113-236.

A major source of mostly first-hand information, with the rest probably coming from contemporary written and oral reports. The author, who seems to have been Luigi Gonzaga, a cousin of the marquess of Mantua, probably stayed in Bologna during at least most of the period of the pope's and emperor's residence. He gives a great deal of information about the processions of the entries and that after the second coronation, as well as about the ceremonies of the coronations. Much less about the *apparati* in the streets. A major source.

4. HOGENBERG, NICOLAS, a series of forty woodcuts showing the procession of the pope and emperor after the second coronation. Copy in the Cabinet des Estampes, Bibliothèque Nationale, Paris: Est. Pd. 21. Several early editions.

None of the early editions seen. Two of them are, however, reproduced in the anonymous *La Coronación imperial de Carlos V* and MAXWELL, *The Procession,* both below.

5. PÉRIL, ROBERT, a series of contemporary engravings showing the procession of the pope and the emperor after the second coronation. The only original copy is said by Jacquot, below, to be in the Cabinet des Estampes of Antwerp. Jacquot mentions a 1579 new edition in the Cabinet des Estampes of the Bibliothèque Nationale, Paris: Est. Pd. 21 +.

Not seen. Jacquot, below, reproduces part of the 1579 edition.

6. RICCHI, AGOSTINO, *Comedia di Agostino Ricchi da Lucca, intittolata i tre tiranni. Recitata in Bologna a N. Signore et a Cesare, il giorno de la commemoratione de la corona di Sua Maesta.* Venezia, Bernardino de' Vitali 1533, 4°, pp. 142. Biblioteca Nazionale, Rome: 69.3.A.59. British Museum, London: 11715, d. 26.

The comedy, with a preface by Alessandro Vellutello in which the circumstances of the production are recalled.

7. SANTA CRUZ, *Crónica del Emperador Carlos V*, vol. III, pp. 67-90.

By the would-be Spanish historiographer of the emperor. A great deal of information on the entry of Charles and on the two coronations and following procession. The author was probably not present but must have had access to contemporary Spanish official sources.

8. SANUDO, *Diarii*, vol. LII, cols. 142-145, 180-199, 205-206, 259-275, 604-619, and 624-682.

A very large number of letters sent to Venice recounting the two entries and the two coronations, with many interesting details. A letter in cols. 259-268 has rather precise descriptions of the *apparati* for the entry of the emperor.

9. VANDENESSE, *Journal des voyages de Charles-Quint*, pp. 85-94.

By a member of the emperor's household staff, a rather full account of the processions and coronations, with, however, no attention to *apparati*.

10. VASARI, in the lives of Alfonso Lombardi Ferrarese and Amico Aspertini (Bagnacavallo) and in his own, *Opere*, vol. V, pp. 84 and 181, and vol. VII, p. 652.

States that Lombardi did the decoration at the door of San Petronio for the imperial coronation and that he did the reliefs for an arch in front of the palace designed by Aspertini. Records also that he himself, as a boy of nineteen, was present and had the occasion to work on some of the *apparati*.

Studies

11. ANONYMOUS, *La Coronación imperial de Carlos V*, edición realizada bajo el patrocinio de la Junta Nacional del IV Centenario. Madrid 1958 (« Collección Joyas Bibliográficas, serie commemorativa », 4), pp. xix-102.

A very handsome folio publication of a sixteenth-century Spanish translation, by Diego Gracián, of a Latin text prescribing the form of the imperial coronation (written before the event) and reproduction of the woodcuts of Hogenberg, above, from a copy in the Biblioteca Nacional of Madrid that is different from that used by Maxwell, below. The anonymous editor provides a short introduction.

12. CONSTANT, G., *Les Maîtres de cérémonies au XVIe siècle: leurs diares*. « Ecole Française de Rome: Mélanges d'Archéologie et d'Histoire », vol. XXIII, 1903, pp. 170-172.

Quotes, with some commentary, several passages from the diary of papal master of ceremonies Biagio da Cesena concerning his arrangements for the proceedings in Bologna.

13. GIORDANI, GAETANO, *Della venuta e dimora in Bologna del Sommo Pontefice Clemente VII. per la coronazione di Carlo V. imperatore celebrata l'anno MDXXX, cronaca con note, documenti ed incisioni*. Bologna, Tip. Governativa Alla Volpe 1842. The book has three sections with separate paginations: *Cronaca*, pp. 184; *Note*, pp. 176; and *Documenti*, pp. 196 and 12 plates.

An extraordinary early example of a major study devoted to a single festive occasion. The *Cronaca* is a painstaking reconstruction of the events, based on a very large number of printed sources (with the notable exceptions of Gonzaga, Sanudo, and Santa Cruz, here listed, which were then still unpublished) and on a number of ms. ones, the chief of the latter being the *Annali di Bologna* of Giovan Francesco Negri. The notes to the *Cronaca* have a vast amount of subsidiary information about people of the time and contain many bibliographical references. The *Documenti* include sixty-three letters and other pieces having to do with the occasion, many of them otherwise unpublished. Some are actual accounts of the entries and coronations (which we do not list separately here). There are also an extensive bibliography of Charles V, with a valuable section on the festivals of his reign, and a list of works of art having to do with him. Twelve plates include portraits of people concerned in the events, illustrations of the costumes of the times, some views of San Petronio and the Piazza Maggiore, and the reproduction of a fresco in the Palazzo Communale depicting the second coronation. This remarkable book is still the first work to be consulted about the festive events of 1529-30.

14. GOETGHEBUER, P. J., *Sur l'entrée de l'Empereur Charles-Quint à Bologne en 1529*, extrait du *Messager des Sciences Historiques de Belgique*. Gand, L. Hebbelynck 1855, pp. 23.

Reproduces thirteen of Hogenberg's engravings, taken from a Flemish edition, with four pages of Flemish text, and provides his own short summary of the entry.

15. JACQUOT, *Panorama des fêtes et cérémonies du règne*, pp. 418-425 and plates I and II at end of volume.

An excellent careful analysis of the entries and coronations, with special attention to the *apparati* and symbolic details of the ceremonies. Based on all the important sources. Reproduces an engraving of Péril showing the pope and emperor riding together after the second coronation and one of Hogenberg showing the distribution of bread to the crowd.

16. MANGO, *La commedia in lingua nel Cinquecento. pp. 100-102*.

Description of the first edition of the comedy (above), mention of the first production, and a bibliography on the work.

17. MAXWELL, SIR WILLIAM STIRLING, *The Entry of the Emperor Charles V into the City of Bologna on the Fifth of November MDXXIX, Reproduced from a Series of Engravings on Wood Printed at Venice in MDXXX.* Privately printed for Sir William Stirling Maxwell at Florence. London and Edinburgh 1875, pp. 8 and 16 double plates.

A reproduction of the engravings of the anonymous *Cavalcata*, above, with a short account of the entry by the author. The engravings show the most important personages of the procession, including the emperor in full battle dress, but no real *apparati*.

18. MAXWELL, SIR WILLIAM STIRLING, *The Procession of Pope Clement VII and the Emperor Charles V after the Coronation of Bologna on the 24th February, MDXXX, Designed and Engraved by Nicolas Hogenberg and Now Reproduced in Facsimile with an Introduction.* Edinburgh, Edmonston and Douglas, George Waterson and Son; London, Hamilton Adams and Co.; Paris, J. Rothschild; Amsterdam, Frederick Muller 1875, pp. 30 and 40 plates.

Reproduces Hogenberg's engravings of the long post-coronation procession and some engravings showing a commemorative fresco in the Palazzo Ridolfi of Verona done by Domenico del Riccio (« il Brusasorzi »). The editor provides an excellent historical introduction, treating events both preceding and following the coronations, and giving information about works of art inspired by the occasion.

19. MUZZI, *Annali della città di Bologna*, vol. VI, pp. 238-443.

An extended account of the pope's and the emperor's visit to Bologna, with a great deal of information on all important events. Detailed description of the *apparati* for Charles' entry and for the second coronation with the text of many inscriptions. Speculation (pp. 249-250) on which artists were resident in the city and must have worked on the *apparati*. A major compendium of information on the occasion, presumably based on ms. sources, though there are no notes.

20. PASTOR, *Storia dei papi*, vol. IV, parte I, pp. 353-366.

A very good short account of the occasion, with many bibliographical references. Little attention, however, to the *apparati*.

21. RINALDI, *Annales ecclesiastici*, tomus XIII, pp. 121-122 and 129-140.

A rather full account with long quotations from the ms. diary of Biagio da Cesena, papal master of ceremonies, which has particularly detailed information about the coronations. Use and quotation as well of some other sources.

22. RODOCANACHI, EMMANUEL, *Histoire de Rome: les pontificats d'Adrien VI et de Clément VII.* Paris, Hachette 1933, pp. 240-245.

A good summary of events with attention to the ceremonies of the coronations.

23. RODRIGUEZ-MOÑINO, A., *Vasco Díaz témoin et chroniqueur poétique du couronnement de Charles-Quint*. In JACQUOT, *Les Fêtes de la Renaissance II*, pp. 183-195.

Discusses verse accounts of the two coronations done by a Spanish gentleman present in Bologna. Some interesting details.

24. STRONG, *Splendour at Court*, pp. 86-91 and plates 67-71.

A summary of events with particular attention to the entry of the emperor. Reproduction of four woodcuts from the anonymous *Cavalcata*, above, and of one from Hogenberg's procession after the coronation.

25. RUSCONI, CARLO, *L'incoronazione di Carlo V a Bologna*, 2ª ed. riveduta e corretta dall'autore. Torino, G. Favale 1859, pp. 504.

A historical novel by an anti-clerical writer of the Risorgimento. Much information about the real events in Bologna alongside fictional episodes.

26. SANESI, *La commedia*, vol. I, pp. 324-328.

An excellent analysis of the play with mention of the circumstances of the first production.

27. TERLINDEN, VICOMTE, *La Politique italienne de Charles Quint et le « Triomphe » de Bologne*. In JACQUOT, *Les Fêtes de la Renaissance II*, pp. 29-43.

An excellent study of the political significance of the events in Bologna, with summaries of the principal ceremonies based in large part on a contemporary pamphlet in Flemish by which Charles had personally informed his subjects in the Low Countries of his coronations.

28. VIZANI, *Historie della sua patria*, pp. 540-556.

A long account of the occasion with much information on Charles' entry, on the two coronations, and on the following procession.

CREMONA

I

1509, June 24. Triumphal Entry of King Louis XII of France after Victories over the Venetians That Have Made Him Lord of the City.

The king entered by the Porta d'Ognissanti, after having been met by a delegation of noble young men of the city, and proceeded under a *baldacchino* to the Duomo and then to the palace of Ludovico Trecco, where he was to stay. Principal *apparati*: at the Gate, a figure representing the city in an attitude of reverence, a Peace and a Justice; at San Prospero, a triumphal arch with inscriptions comparing the king to Caesar; at San Matteo, another arch with inscriptions; at Sant'Elena, an arch with inscriptions; at San Leonardo, an arch with inscriptions; and at Piazza Sant'Agata, the principal arch with inscriptions and statues representing the virtues of the king. Dominico Bordigallo, author of a ms. chronicle, is said to have been in charge of planning the *apparati*. The artists seem to be unknown and apparently no drawings survive, but there are good descriptions, and the inscriptions are recorded.

Sources

1. Alfeni, Carlo, *Narratione dell'entrata in Cremona di Lodovico XII re di Francia* [...], published by « F.N. » below.

A systematic, detailed account that is the source of most of our information.

2. Marot de Caen, *Les deux heureux voyages de Genes et Venise*, cc. 118r-120v.

A witness account in affected *grand rhétoriqueur* verse, with general allusions to the *apparati* and the text of one inscription.

3. « F.N. », *Una visita di Luigi XII alla città di Cremona (24-26 giugno 1509).*
« Archivio Storico Lombardo », serie 4ª, vol. VIII, anno XXXIV, 1907, pp. 152-
166.

Publishes a ms. account of the entry by Carlo Alfeni, above, with numerous com-
parisons to other sources, notably the ms. report of Dominico Bordigallo (who is said
by Alfeni to have been in charge of the preparations). Alfeni's narrative includes good
descriptions of the *apparati* and the text of a number of inscriptions.

II

1549, January 10. ENTRY OF PRINCE PHILLIP OF SPAIN, ON HIS WAY
TO AUSTRIA, GERMANY, AND THE LOW COUNTRIES.

A poorly known entry. There were three triumphal arches, of
which some description survives and whose inscriptions welcoming
the prince are recorded. The *apparati* apparently included an allusion
to the neo-Latin poet Girolamo Vida, a native son of whom the city
was said to have been as proud as Mantua of Vergil.

Sources

1. CALVETE, *El felicissimo viaje*, cc. 35r-36r.

By the historian of the prince's journey, the best account with mention of the
apparati and the text of inscriptions.

2. SANTA CRUZ, *Crónica del Emperador Carlos Quintos*, vol. V.

Not seen. Since the earlier volumes of this work have good accounts of preceding
imperial state occasions, it is possible there is information on this one as well.

3. ULLOA, *Vita e fatti dell' [...] imperatore Carlo Quinto*, c. 186r.

A short account by a possible witness with a vague reference to the *apparati*.

Study

4. NICOLINI, *Sul viaggio di Filippo d'Asburgo in Italia*, p. 260.

A brief report of the prince's passage.

FERRARA

I

1502, February 1-8. Celebrations for the Arrival of Lucrezia Borgia, Daughter of Pope Alexander VI and New Bride of Alfonso d'Este, Son of Duke Ercole I.

On February 1 Alfonso went in the Bucentaur to fetch his bride at the Torre di Fosso and bring her to a palace just outside the city. February 2: entry of Lucrezia into the the city by the Ponte di Castel Tedaldo and procession by a roundabout route, past the church of San Domenico and the Palazzo Schifanoia, to the Duomo and the Castello, where the bride was welcomed by Isabella d'Este. Along the way there were at least four stages from which actors, many of them representing mythological characters, recited verses to the bride. (The verses are not recorded). On the following days five comedies of Plautus in Italian translation were played in a very large room of the Palazzo della Ragione, which had been specially prepared. February 3: the *Epidicus*; February 4: the *Bacchidi*; February 5: the *Miles gloriosus*; February 7: the *Asinaria*; and February 8: the *Cassina*. All the comedies had *intermedii* with dancing and very elaborate costumes. The productions occupy an important place in theatre history.

Sources

1. Anonymous, *Diario ferrarese dall'anno 1409 sino al 1502*, a cura di Giuseppe Pardi. In Muratori, *Rerum italicarum scriptores*, tomo XXIV, parte VII, pp. 280-285.

A good first-hand account, though it is in general less detailed than that of Zambotti, below.

2. ESTE, ISABELLA D', seven letters written from Ferrara to her husband the marquess of Mantua during the wedding celebrations, published by Carlo d'Arco in his *Notizie di Isabella d'Estense moglie a Francesco Gonzaga, aggiuntivi molti documenti che si riferiscono alla stessa signora, all'historia di Mantova, ed a quella generale d'Italia,* « Archivio Storico Italiano », appendice II, 1845, pp. 300-310.

A good deal of information on the playing of the comedies and other entertainments. One or more of the letters are cited in several of the studies of the festival listed below.

3. SANUDO, *Diarii,* vol. IV, cols. 222-230.

Publishes a systematic *Ordine di le pompe e spectaculi di le nozze di Madona Lucrezia Borgia* which contains a great deal of information about all the festivities, including the productions of the comedies and their *intermedii.* A major source.

4. SARDI, *Libro delle historie ferraresi,* p. 198 in Sardi's section of the book.

A laconic recording of Lucrezia's arrival in Ferrara.

5. ZAMBOTTI, BERNARDINO, *Diario ferrarese dall'anno 1476 al 1504,* a cura di Giuseppe Pardi. In MURATORI, *Rerum italicarum scriptores,* tomo XXIV, parte VII, pp. 311-338.

Very detailed accounts of the entry and of the later entertainments. Zambotti's own report occupies pp. 312-318 and 333-338. Pp. 318-331 contain an account of the activities of the French ambassador for the occasion written by his secretary Niccolo Cagnola. Both have a great deal of information about the playing of the comedies. The main source.

Studies

6. CREIZENACH, *Geschichte des Neueren Dramas,* Band II, Theil I, p. 222.

A short report of the comedy productions with a reference to Isabella d'Este's impressions.

7. COPPI, ANNA MARIA, *Spettacoli alla corte di Ercole I,* in *Pubblicazioni dell'Università Cattolica del Sacro Cuore,* contributi, serie 3ª, scienze filologiche e letteratura, 17, contributi dell'Istituto di Filologia Moderna. Milano, Vita e Pensiero 1968 (« Storia del teatro », 1), pp. 38 and 58.

A short account of the playing of the comedies with publication of a passage from the ms. chronicle of Fra Paolo da Legnazzo reporting the productions.

8. D'ANCONA, *Origini del teatro italiano,* vol. II, pp. 134-135 and 383-387.

Examinations of the productions of the comedies with long quotations of descriptive letters Isabella d'Este wrote to her husband the Marquess of Mantua.

9. *Enciclopedia dello spettacolo*, under « Ferrara », vol. V, p. 175.

A good deal of information about the production of the comedies and about their *intermedii*.

10. FRIZZI, *Memorie per la storia di Ferrara*, vol. IV, pp. 205-208.

A good summary of events.

11. GREGOROVIUS, *Lucrezia Borgia*, pp. 233-254 and 347-355.

A very good account, with many quotations from letters and diaries. This edition also reproduces the report in Sanudo, above.

12. LUZIO, ALESSANDRO, and RENIER, RODOLFO, *Mantova e Urbino, Isabella d'Este Gonzaga nelle relazioni familiari e nelle vicende politiche.* Torino-Roma, L. Roux 1893, pp. 113-116.

An interesting account of the visit of Isabella d'Este and her sister-in-law Elisabetta Gonzaga to Ferrara for the celebrations, with the former's reaction to the production of the comedies.

13. MURATORI, *Delle antichità estensi continuazione*, p. 274.

A short account of Lucrezia's arrival and later entertainments.

14. PIRROTTA, *Li due Orfei*, pp. 58-63.

A consideration of the comedy productions, with quotations from sources, and speculation about the nature of the music for the *intermedii*.

15. POVOLEDO, *Origini e aspetti della scenografia in Italia*, pp. 363-364, 366-367, and 370.

A careful and valuable study of all that is known of the scenography for the comedies.

16. ZORZI, *Il teatro e la città*, pp. 19-20, 46, 97-98, and 198.

Short examinations of the productions of the comedies, with quotation of a letter in which Isabella d'Este gives her impressions.

II

1528, December 1, and the following weeks. ENTRY OF RENÉE DE FRANCE, NEW BRIDE OF THE FUTURE DUKE ERCOLE II D'ESTE, AND LATER ENTERTAINMENTS.

The princess, who had earlier been lavishly entertained in Modena, spent one night at the Palazzo del Belvedere, on the Po, and then came to the city in the Bucentaur on December 1. She entered by the Porta San Paolo, under a *baldacchino*, with an elaborate procession. She was greeted at the Castello by Isabella d'Este. The street *apparati* seem to have been simple. Ludovico Ariosto's comedy *La Lena* was played soon after the duchess' arrival, and on January 24 there was a lavish banquet with a playing of his *Cassaria*. *Il negromante* was apparently also put on during the carnival season.

Sources

1. MESSISBUGO, CRISTOFORO DI, *Banchetti, compositioni et apparecchio generale* [...]. Ferrara, Giovanni De Bughat et Antonio Hucher 1549, cc. 4v-8r. Biblioteca Nazionale, Florence: Palat. (14) X 7.4.15. Reproduced partly by Fontana, below.

In a manual for princely entertaining, the author recalls a banquet given by Ercole d'Este to his father on January 24, 1529. There are a complete list of the courses served and a short account of the playing of *La cassaria*, which immediately preceded the banquet.

2. SARDI, *Libro delle historie ferraresi*, pp. 7-8.

A short account of the entry with some description of the decorations and procession.

Studies

3. D'ANCONA, *Origini del teatro italiano*, vol. II, pp. 137 and 429-430.

Mentions the production of *La cassaria*, with a reference to Messisbugo, and quotes a letter addressed to the Marquess of Mantua stating that a production of Plautus' *Menaechmi* was also being prepared.

4. *Enciclopedia dello spettacolo*, under « Ferrara », vol. V, col. 177.

States that Ariosto's *Il negromante*, as well as *La Lena* and the *Cassaria*, was produced during the prolonged celebrations.

5. FONTANA, *Renata di Francia*, vol. I, pp. 74-99.

By far the best account of the entry and later entertainments, with quotations of several ms. sources and of Messisbugo.

6. FRIZZI, *Memorie per la storia di Ferrara*, vol. IV, pp. 305-307.

A short account with some particular information on the preparations.

7. MANGO, *La commedia in lingua nel Cinquecento*, pp. 92-94 and 103-105.

Description of the first editions of the three comedies, short analyses of their plots, information about the first productions, and short bibliographies.

8. MURATORI, *Delle antichità estensi continuazione*, p. 353.

A summary of the entry with mention of later entertainments.

9. RODOCANACHI, *Une protectrice de la Réforme*, pp. 52-55.

A summary of events apparently derived largely from Fontana, above.

10. SANESI, *La Commedia*, vol. I, pp. 222-230 and 234-241.

Analyses of the three Ariosto comedies, with information about their composition and about their early productions.

III

1543, April 21-25. ENTRY AND SOJOURN OF POPE PAUL III, RETURNING FROM A VISIT TO PARMA AND PIACENZA.

Duke Ercole II of Ferrara had recently been reconciled with the pope, after disputes over the possession of Modena, and it was resolved to make the reception particularly magnificent. The duke sent his Bucentaur up the Po to fetch the pontiff, who was brought to the Palazzo del Belvedere, on an island in the river near Ferrara, on April 21. The next day the duke accompanied the pope in the Bucentaur (presumably on a canal) to the city. The pope entered at

San Giorgio, probably today's Porta Romana, and proceeded to the Duomo and then to the Castello. There were five arches, including one at the city gate and one at the Duomo. Their content is not described in printed sources, but some inscriptions, in praise of the pope, are preserved. On Aprile 24 there was a joust in front of the castello and, in the evening, a playing of Terence's comedy *Adelchi* with the duke's five children acting roles. April 25: departure of the pontiff in the Bucentaur toward Bologna.

Source

1. ANONYMOUS, *Lettera nuova de tutte le entrate feste giostre comedie e doni per la venuta di P.P. III a Ferrara cosa molto bella.* N.p., n.d., but probably Ferrara 1543, 4°, cc. 8. Bibliothèque de l'Arsenal, Paris: Fonds Rondel Ra.[5] 461.

A systematic account in a conversational and witty style, apparently addressed to a prelate in Rome who is the author's brother. Much information on the pope's entry and later activities, a fair amount of description of the *apparati*, with some inscriptions (including two in Greek), and a most interesting account of the production of the comedy, for which are given not only the names of the actors (the duke's children) but also those of the musicians.

Studies

2. *Enciclopedia dello spettacolo*, under « Ferrara », vol. V, col. 177.

States that Giraldi Cinthio's tragedy *Altile* was to have been performed for the pope but that the murder of one of the actors made it necessary to substitute the *Adelchi* played by the duke's children.

3. FONTANA, *Renata di Francia*, vol. II, pp. 177-184.

An excellent modern account with the publication of a Vatican document prescribing the order of the entry and long quotation of a ms. *Ordine dell'intrata di Papa Paolo III in Ferrara* by Giovan Francesco Firmani. Unfortunately the author omits from the latter a section recording the inscriptions of the arches and, perhaps, describing their iconographical content.

4. FRIZZI, *Memorie per la storia di Ferrara*, vol. IV, pp. 341-342.

A short summary of events during the pope's visit.

5. MURATORI, *Delle antichità estensi continuazione*, pp. 367-368.

Good description of the entry and mention of the later entertainments.

3

6. SARDI, *Libro delle historie ferraresi*, pp. 18-21 in the continuation by Faustini.

Good description of the entry, with some information on the *apparati*, and mention of the later entertainments.

7. RODOCANACHI, *Une protectrice de la Réforme*, pp. 160-163.

A useful summary of events during the pope's visit.

FLORENCE

I

1494, November 17-28. ENTRY AND SOJOURN OF KING CHARLES VIII OF FRANCE, ON HIS WAY TO CONQUER THE KINGDOM OF NAPLES.

Quite an elaborate entry, though the decorations and other preparations were done rather hurriedly after the expulsion of Piero de' Medici and the reluctant decision of the republican Signoria to receive the king and his army. Entry by the Porta San Frediano, with important *apparati* there, at Piazza Frescobaldi, Ponte Vecchio, Piazza della Signoria (with a « Triumph of Peace » by Filippino Lippi), Piazza San Giovanni, Palazzo Medici (with a triumphal arch by Pietro Perugino), and the house of Pierfrancesco de' Medici. The king stayed at the Palazzo Medici. November 23: performance of a *sacra rappresentazione* of the Annunciation in the king's presence at San Felice. November 26: swearing to a treaty between the king and the Signoria after a mass in the Duomo. No drawings of *apparati* survive, though there are simple woodcuts inspired by the entry (see La Vigne, below). Verbal descriptions are not very detailed. Among artists, besides Lippi and Perugino, who worked on the *apparati*: Antonio di Jacopo, Andrea di Salvi, Luca di Frosino, and, perhaps, Antonio da San Gallo the Elder, his brother Giuliano, and the sculptor called Ciatto.

Sources

1. CAMBI, *Istorie*, tomo II, pp. 80-82.

An account with few details by a probable witness.

2. Desrey, *Relation du voyage du roi Charles VIII*, in Godefroy ed., p. 204; in Cimber ed., pp. 220-221.

A short account of the entry by a witness.

3. Gaddi, Agnolo and Francesco, *Sulla cacciata di Piero de' Medici, e la venuta di Carlo VIII in Firenze; estratto dal* Priorista *di Agnolo e Francesco Gaddi.* Published by an anonymous editor in « Archivio Storico Italiano », tomo IV, parte II, 1853, pp. 41-49.

Much information on negotiations and arrangements before the king's entry, some on the procession, none on decorations.

4. Guicciardini, Francesco, *Storie fiorentine dal 1378 al 1509*, a cura di Roberto Palmarocchi. Bari, Laterza 1931 (« Scrittori d'Italia », 134), pp. 102-112.

A good amount of information on the entry, which the author probably witnessed.

5. Landucci, *Diario*, pp. 79-87.

By a witness, some information about the *apparati*, much about the mood and reactions of the Florentines during the sojourn of the king and his army.

6. Lapini, *Diario fiorentino*, pp. 28-30.

A personal account with, however, no information on the procession or the *apparati*.

7. La Vigne, *Vergier d'honneur*, ca. 1500 ed., cc. g4r-h2v, largely reprinted in Roscoe, *Vita e pontificato di Leon X*, vol. III, pp. 272-283; *Histoire du voyage de Naples*, pp. 118-120; *La Très Curieuse et Chevaleresque Hystoire de la conqueste de Naples*, pp. 43-47.

By the king's historiographer, who was present, detailed descriptions of the procession. There is little description of the *apparati*, but the ca. 1500 ed. of the *Vergier* has five simple woodcuts that apparently recall the « hystoires sur les eschaffaulx de Florence ». These woodcuts do not seem to have been examined by modern students of the entry.

8. Masi, *Ricordanze*, pp. 24-27.

A witness account with the exact route of the procession and mention of *apparati* at the Piazza San Giovanni.

9. Nardi, *Istorie*, vol. I, pp. 36-46.

By a witness who was, however, writing years after the events. Few details about the *apparati*, much about the negociations between the king and the Signoria.

10. SANUDO, *La spedizione di Carlo VIII*, pp. 131-136.

Includes a long quotation from the account of a witness. One of the best sources for details of the decorations, much also on the costumes and the procession.

Studies

11. BORSOOK, EVE, *Décor in Florence for the Entry of Charles VIII of France.* « Mitteilungen des Kunsthistorischen Instituts in Florenz », Band X, Heft II, 1961, pp. 106-122.

An excellent summary of the entry, with numerous quotations from printed sources and also from the ms. *Istorie* of P. Parenti and *Sommario* [...] *delle cose di Firenze* of B. Cerretani. Transcription of the records of payments to artists in the Florentine Archivio di Stato. Reproductions (1) of a Bible frontispiece that seems to evoke the entry and (2) of a medal struck by the Florentines to commemorate the king's visit. Careful analysis to what is known of the decorations, with allusions to other works of Lippi and Perugino. Precise documentation. The principal and best study of this entry.

12. BORSOOK, EVE, *Addendum to the Entry of Charles VIII*. « Mitteilungen des Kunsthistorischen Instituts in Florenz », Band X, Heft III, 1962, p. 217.

The author takes cognizance of Labande's earlier study, below, which she had not known before.

13. CHARTROU, *Les Entrées solennelles et triomphales à la Renaissance*, pp. 74-75.

A small amount of information on the entry, based on La Vigne.

14. CHERRIER, *Histoire de Charles VIII*, vol. II, pp. 28-33.

A good short summary of the entry with much on the procession and something on the *apparati*.

15. DELABORDE, *L'Expédition de Charles VIII en Italie*, pp. 445-485.

A good summary of the entry, based on most of the sources, and a detailed scholarly account of the negotiations between the king and the Signoria.

16. LABANDE, YVONNE, *L'Entrée de Charles VIII à Florence (17 novembre 1494)*. « Etudes Italiennes », nouvelle série, tome V, 1935, pp. 31-43.

A good summary of the entry with particular attention to the procession. Little description of the *apparati*. Documentation of quotations and information is not always precise, but there is a bibliography.

17. PERRENS, *Histoire de Florence*, tome II, pp. 94-109.

A good account of events during the king's stay with little attention to the entry itself.

II

1513, February 6-8. CARNIVAL PARADES WITH MOTIFS CELEBRATING THE RETURN OF THE MEDICI, SEVERAL MONTHS BEFORE.

Extremely elaborate celebrations with the contributions of leading artists and letterati. Giuliano de' Medici, brother of Cardinal Giovanni de' Medici, soon to be elected pope, and Lorenzo de' Medici, the cardinal's nephew, organized rival companies called « Il Diamante » and « Il Broncone » (after Medici devices) in order to prepare the parades. That for the Broncone, on February 6, was planned by Jacopo Nardi and included chariots representing the « Seven Triumphs of the Golden Age »: (1) the Golden Age of Saturn, (2) the Age of Numa Pomphilus, (3) the Age of Titus Manlius Torquatus, (4) the Age of Julius Caesar, (5) the Age of Caesar Augustus, (6) the Age of Trajan, and (7) the Return of the Golden Age. The last chariot, showing a withered laurel branch putting forth new leaves, clearly alluded to the return of the Medici. Nardi, the planner, also wrote a poem, « I sette trionfi del secol d'oro », for recitation. The parade of the Diamante, on February 8, was planned by the classical scholar Andrea Dazzi. It included chariots representing the « Three Ages of Man »: Pueritia, Virilitas, and Senectus. Antonio Alamanni had written a poem called « Trionfo dell'età dell'uomo ». Artists known to have worked on the *apparati*: Il Pontormo and Baccio Bandinelli (on the floats of the Broncone), Andrea del Sarto, Andrea di Cosimo Feltrini, Raffaello delle Vivuole, and the wood-carver Carota (on those of the Diamante). The poetry survives, as do some preparatory drawings for the *apparati* and some actual chiaroscuro canvases for the floats. (See Shearman, below).

Sources

1. ALAMANNI, ANTONIO, his poem « Trionfo dell'età dell'uomo ». In SINGLETON, CHARLES, editor, *Canti carnascialeschi del Rinascimento*, Bari, Laterza 1936 (« Scrittori d'Italia », 159), pp. 240-241.

2. CAMBI, *Istorie*, vol. III, pp. 2-3.

A disapproving but very interesting account by an opponent of the Medici who thought the celebrations were inappropriate.

3. NARDI, JACOPO, his poem « I setti trionfi del secol d'oro ». In SINGLETON, *Canti carnascialeschi del Rinascimento*, cited above, pp. 251-253.

4. NARDI, *Istoria di Firenze*, vol. II, pp. 16-17.

A short account with no mention of the author's own involvement.

5. VASARI, in his life of Pontormo, *Opere*, vol. VI, pp. 250-255.

A great deal of information on the *apparati*, and quotation of Nardi's poem. Erroneously associates the celebrations with the election of Leo X, which came shortly afterward. The main source.

Studies

6. BURCKHARDT, *La civiltà del Rinascimento in Italia*, vol. II, pp. 182-183.

In the author's famous chapter on Renaissance festivals, a good description of the parades, which, following Vasari, he erroneously connects with the election of Leo X.

7. *Enciclopedia dello spettacolo*, under « Firenze », vol. V, col. 376.

A short discussion of the celebrations, which, following Vasari, are wrongly associated with Leo X.

8. SHEARMAN, JOHN, *Pontorno and Andrea del Sarto, 1513*. « Burlington Magazine », vol. CIV, 1962, pp. 478-483.

A thorough study of the works of art commissioned for the festival, based on ms. as well as printed sources. The author reproduces two chiaroscuro canvases from the Kress Collection of Bucknell University that he believes survive from a chariot, a drawing that seems to be preparatory for that chariot, and two drawings of Andrea del Sarto that he associates with other chariots. Careful documentation.

III

1515, November 30-December 3. ENTRY AND SOJOURN OF POPE LEO X, EN ROUTE TO MEET KING FRANCIS OF FRANCE IN BOLOGNA.

The Florentines were welcoming a native son, Giovanni de' Medici, and the entry was a particularly magnificent one, with elaborate *apparati* in the route of the procession and special decoration of the Sala del Papa at Santa Maria Novella. Eight triumphal arches (of which one formed a temporary decade of the Duomo), representing the seven canonical virtues individually and all of them together. Also an obelisk, a storied column, a «castello», and colossal statues of a horse and of Hercules. Choirs at the principal *apparati* sang explanatory verses, and there were probably also *tableaux vivants*, or dramatic skits acted out on the pope's passage. The extremely elaborate procession, which included Roman officials in the pope's company, foreign ambassadors, and Florentine dignitaries, entered at the Porta San Piero Gattolini (today's Porta Romana), and passed by San Felice in Piazza, the Ponte Santa Trinita, the Bargello, the Badia Fiorentina, the Duomo, the Baptistry, and the Canto de' Carnesecchi to Santa Maria Novella, where the pontiff was to stay in the Sala del Papa. Among the artists who worked on the decorations: Andrea del Sarto, Baccio Bandinelli, Jacopo Sansovino, either Antonio da San Gallo the Elder or Bernardino da San Gallo, Bastiano (Aristotele) da San Gallo, Baccio da Montelupo, Francesco Granacci, Rosso Fiorentino, Ridolfo Ghirlandaio, Giovanfrancesco Rustici, Jacopo da Pontormo, Andrea de' Feltrini, Piero da Sesto, Giuliano Bugiardini, Piero di Cosimo, Perino del Vaga, Toto della Nunziata, and Jacopo da Bonaccorso. The music performed for the entry is apparently not identified, and the verses do not seem to have survived. Practically no works of art survive (see Pope-Hennessy and Shearman, below), but there is a great deal of written description and documentation. Vasari's Palazzo Vecchio fresco showing the procession as it passed through the Piazza della Signoria also contains accurate information.

Sources

1. ANONYMOUS, pages from a diary in Italian reproduced by Moreni in his edition of Grassi, below, pp. 9-12, and in ROSCOE, *Vita e pontificato di Leon X*, vol. VI, pp. 280-283.

This short description, which Shearman, in *Entrata*, below, says relies on Panciatichi, records five inscriptions.

2. ANONYMOUS, *Archi, et spectaculi preparati a Fiorenza per la entrata di Papa Leone X^{mo} del anno 1515*. A ms. published by Shearman, in *Entrata*, below, pp. 144-148.

A program for the decorations, written in the future tense, explaining the symbolism of eight arches. There is no mention of the obelisk, the « castello », the storied column, or the colossal statues, all of which may have been late additions to the plans.

3. CAMBI, *Istorie*, tomo III, pp. 81-88.

Enumeration of the *apparati* with little description. Much attention to the procession and costumes, which the author observed from an official seat near the Badia.

4. CHIERIGATO, FRANCESCO, *Descriptione de la entrata de la Sta di N.S. Papa Leone X^{mo} in la citta di Fiorenza significata per lo R^{do} M. Franc^o Chierigatto alla Illma et Exma madamma nostra: la quale fu a di xxx di novembre M.D.XV*. Published by Shearman in *Entrata*, below, pp. 148-153.

A letter of description addressed to Isabella d'Este in Mantua, with attention mainly to the procession and costumes.

5. GRASSI, PARIDE DE', *De Ingressu Summi Pont. Leonis X. Florentiam Descriptio Paridis De Grassis Civis Bononiensis Pisaurensis Episcopi*, ex cod. ms. nunc primum in lucem edita et notis illustrata a Dominico Moreni Accademiae nec non Columbariae socio. Florentiae, apud Caietanum Cambiagi 1793, 8°, pp. 56. Biblioteca Nazionale, Florence: 10604.15. This section dealing with the reception is left out of the published *Diario di Leon X*, but much of it, covering events through the first day, is published as well in ROSCOE, *Vita e pontificato di Leone X*, vol. VI, pp. 283-291.

Pages from the diary of Grassi, papal master of ceremonies, who was accompanying the pope. The somewhat ill-tempered account of the entry contains much information about the arrangements for the procession and disputes over precedence in which Grassi intervened. There is little description of *apparati*. The editor provides an introduction and voluminous notes (also in Latin), including material from the then unpublished diary of Landucci, below.

6. LANDUCCI, *Diario fiorentino*, pp. 352-360.

Much description of the *apparati*, with specification of their dimensions. The diarist shows great pride in the expenditures of the Signoria and the accomplishments of Florentine artists. A major source.

7. MASI, *Ricordanze*, pp. 162-176.

Considerable description of the *apparati*, exact notation of the route of the entry, a witness account of ceremonies in Santa Annunziata and San Lorenzo, much discussion of expenses, many peripheral details. A major source.

8. NARDI, *Istorie*, tomo II, pp. 42-43.

An extremely spare account by the man who, according to Shearman, in *Entrata*, below, may have been the principal planner of the celebrations.

9. PANCIATICHI, GUALTIERI, *Copia di una epistola di Gualtieri ciptadino fiorentino nella entrata di Papa Leone. Nella cipta di Firenze. Adi. xxx. di novembre MD.XV*. Firenze, Lionardo di Neri Cartolario, 3 gennaio 1515 (Florentine style).

A rare publication that I have not seen. According to Shearman, in *Entrata*, below, « while tiresomely affected in literary style, it is exceptionally helpful on inscriptions and architectural forms ».

10. SANUDO, *Diarii*, vol. XXI, cols. 374-375.

A letter from the Venetian envoy Marino Zorzi with a good deal of information about the procession and costumes, but only brief mentions of the *apparati*.

11. VASARI, in the lives of Baccio da Montelupo, Andrea del Sarto, Rosso Fiorentino, Andrea de' Feltrini, Francesco Granacci, Perino del Vaga, Baccio Bandinelli, Jacopo da Pontormo, Bastiano (Aristotele) da San Gallo, Ridolfo Ghirlandaio, Giovanfrancesco Rustici, and Jacopo Sansovino, and in his *Ragionamento terzo*, *Opere*, vol. IV, p. 541; vol. V, pp. 24-26, 158, 207-208, 341-342, and 596; vol. VI, pp. 141-142, 255-256, 436, 541, and 602; vol. VII, pp. 494-495; and vol. VIII, pp. 140-145.

A very large amount of information, most of it doubtless accurate, though Vasari himself had not been a witness of the entry. A major source.

Studies

12. PASTOR, *Storia dei papi*, vol. IV, parte I, pp. 83-84.

A summary of the pope's entry and stay, with numerous bibliographical references, including some to mss.

13. PERRENS, *Histoire de Florence*, vol. III, pp. 54-56.

An interesting account of the entry and stay, with information about a dispute between Grassi and the Signoria.

14. POPE-HENNESSY, JOHN, *A Relief by Sansovino*. « Burlington Magazine », vol. CI, 1959, pp. 4-10.

The author describes a relief now in the Victoria and Albert Museum in London which he thinks represents Susanna and the Elders, attributes to Jacopo Sansovino, and suggests may be a survival of the temporary facade of the Duomo constructed for the 1515 entry.

15. RODOCANACHI, *Le Pontificat de Léon X*, pp. 88-89.

A good short summary, with some attention to the *apparati*.

16. ROSCOE, *Vita e pontificato di Leone X*, vol. V, pp. 134-141, and vol. VI, pp. 283-291.

A good account of the entry and sojourn with some description of the *apparati*. Publication of the section of Grassi's diary dealing with the entry.

17. SCHAEFFER, EMIL, *Der Herakles des Baccio Bandinelli*. « Monatshefte für Kunstwissenschaft », Band III, 1910, pp. 112-114.

Speculates on the form of Bandinelli's statue of Hercules, which stood in the Loggia de' Lanzi during the entry. Reproduces Vasari's commemorative fresco in the Palazzo Vecchio.

18. SHEARMAN, JOHN, *Andrea del Sarto*. Oxford, Clarendon Press 1965, vol. II, pp. 317-319 and 392-393.

Discussion of what is known of the temporary facade of the Duomo and the statue of a horse at Piazza Santa Maria Novella.

19. SHEARMAN, JOHN, *The Florentine* Entrata *of Leo X, 1515*. « Journal of the Warburg and Courtauld Institutes », vol. XXXVIII, 1975, pp. 136-154.

Publishes two new ms. documents (listed above). Describes a maiolica dish that commemorates the entry. Analyzes the main iconography of the *apparati*, using all the printed sources and several ms. ones, which are listed and described in a note. Correlates the details of the two new documents with those found in other sources. Has used records o payment to artists in the Florentine Archivio di Stato. This is by far the most importan study of the entry.

IV

1518, September 7-12. FESTIVITIES FOR THE MARRIAGE OF LORENZO DE' MEDICI, DUKE OF URBINO, AND MADELEINE DE LA TOUR D'AUVERGNE, A KINSWOMAN OF KING FRANCIS I OF FRANCE.

Entry of the duchess (who had been married to Lorenzo in France) on September 7, three days of entertainments in the Palazzo Medici, and, on the 12th, homage of the *Potenze* of Florence. Little is known of the street decorations on the route of entry. Entertainments at the Palazzo Medici included the playing of one, two, or perhaps three comedies, one of which may have been *La mandragola* of Machiavelli in first performance. Artists known to have worked on the stage scenery and decorations of the palace: Bastiano (Aristotele) da San Gallo, Ridolfo Ghirlandaio, Andrea di Cosimo de' Feltrini, and Franciabigio.

Sources

1. CAMBI, *Istorie*, tomo III, pp. 141-142.

Gives the route of the entry without description of street decorations. Tells of a *convito* in the garden of the Palazzo Medici but does not mention comedies.

2. MASI, *Ricordanze*, pp. 235-237.

Tells in general terms of decorations at the palace and in Via Larga, and of banquets and dancing. No mention of comedies.

3. MEDICI, ALFONSINA DE' (mother of Duke Lorenzo), letter to Ser Giovanni da Poppi, dated September 8, 1518, published by an anonymous editor as *Le feste celebrate in Firenze nel II giorno delle nozze di Lorenzo de' Medici duca di Urbino e Maddalena della Tour d'Auvergne*. Firenze, Tip. dell'Arte della Bella Stampa 1882, pp. 12 (Nozze Puccini-Manfredi).

Written on the second day of the festivities, the letter tells of that day's banquet and of the playing of one comedy, called « Falargho », which cannot be certainly identified. The main source.

4. SANUDO, *Diarii*, vol. XXVI, cols. 18-19.

Gives the text of a letter from the Venetian ambassador in Rome saying that Lorenzo will make his entry into Florence on September 7 and that all the buffoons in Rome, including the famous « Cherea », have gone to « far commedie » during the celebrations.

5. VASARI, in the lives of Franciabigio, Andrea de' Feltrini, Bastiano (Aristotele) da San Gallo, and Ridolfo Ghirlandaio, *Opere*, vol. V, pp. 195 and 208; vol. VI, pp. 436 and 541-542.

A small amount of information about the *apparati* for the comedies.

Studies

6. BERTELLI, SERGIO, *When Did Machiavelli Write* La Mandragola? « Renaissance Quarterly », vol. XXIV, 1971, pp. 317-326.

Rejects the 1518 dating of the play and suggests, without concluding, that it may have been written either much earlier, in 1504, or later, in 1519.

7. CHIAPPELLI, FREDI, *Sulla composizione della* Mandragola. «L'Approdo Letterario», 1965, pp. 84-97.

Rejects the dating of the comedy in 1518 by Ridolfi and Parronchi, below.

8. FABBRI, MARIO, *Il luogo teatrale*, pp. 73-74 and 80.

Descriptions of ms. copies and early editions of *La mandragola* and the two comedies of Strozzi, with some necessarily hesitant discussion of the 1518 productions. Quotation of Alfonsina de' Medici's letter.

9. GORI, *Firenze magnifica*, pp. 103-110.

Summary of what was known of the celebrations before speculation about the production of *La mandragola*. Quotations of Cambi and Alfonsina de' Medici, above.

10. MANGO, *La commedia in lingua nel Cinquecento*, pp. 70-71, 83-84, and 272-273.

Description of the sixteenth-century mss. of Strozzi's two comedies and of the first edition of *La mandragola*, with summaries of the plays and bibliography.

11. PARRONCHI, ALESSANDRO, *La prima rappresentazione della* Mandragola: *il modello per l'apparato, l'allegoria.* «La Bibliofilia», vol. LXIV, 1962, pp. 37-86.

Taking as his point of departure Ridolfi's dating of the play, below, the author conjectures that it was presented, along with two other comedies, the *Commedia in versi* and *La pisana*, both of Lorenzo Strozzi, for the wedding celebrations of 1518. Very interesting, if uncautious, speculations about the *apparati* for the three productions, which he connects with three paintings of buildings in perspective now in Urbino, Berlin, and Baltimore (reproduced in the article). The author presents as well an elaborate interpretation of *La mandragola* as a political allegory.

12. PIRROTTA, *Li due Orfei*, pp. 145-146 and 191 (note).

Speculation about the original musical *intermedii* of *La mandragola* and a skeptical summary of Parronchi's theory about the *apparati*.

13. POVOLEDO, *Origini e aspetti della scenografia in Italia*, p. 398 (note).

Summarizes and rejects Parronchi's theory about the *apparati*.

14. RIDOLFI, ROBERTO, *Vita di Niccolò Machiavelli*. Roma, Angelo Belardetti 1954, pp. 256-260 and 442-445.

Taking as evidence an allusion in the play to the danger of an imminent Turkish invasion, the author argues that *La mandragola* was written in 1518 and wonders whether it may have been performed for the *nozze* of Lorenzo and Madeleine.

15. Ridolfi, Roberto, *Composizione, rappresentazione e prima edizione della* Mandragola. « La Bibliofilia », vol. LXIV, 1962, pp. 285-300.

In reply to Parronchi's article, above, the author expresses doubts about the allegorical interpretation of the comedy and suggests that it may have been written early in 1518 and performed for the carnival of that year.

16. Sanesi, *La commedia*, vol. I, pp. 250-252.

Analyses of *La mandragola* and Strozzi's two comedies.

V

1536, April 29. Entry of the Emperor Charles V, during His Triumphal Progress up the Peninsula after the Victory of Tunis.

An extremely elaborate entry by the Porta San Pietro Gattolini (Porta Romana), with progress by the Canto alla Cuculia, San Felice, Via Maggio, the Ponte Santa Trinita, Piazza Santa Trinita, Canto de' Tornaquinci, Canto de' Carnesecchi, Canto alla Paglia, the Duomo, Piazza San Giovanni, and Via de' Martelli to the Palazzo Medici, where the emperor was to stay. Charles, who was accompanied by Francesco Guicciardini, was met at the gate by Duke Alessandro de' Medici and city officials. Principal *apparati* on the route of the procession: Charles' device of two columns at the gate, a triumphal arch at the Canto alla Cuculia, a temporary facade of San Felice, a statue of Hercules in the Via Maggio, statues of rivers at the bridge, an unfinished equestrian statue of Charles at the Piazza Santa Trinita, a statue of Jason in the Canto de' Carnesecchi, three theological Virtues over the portal of the Duomo, statues of Prudence and Justice in the Via de' Martelli, and decoration of the Medici Palace. The tone of the decorations definitely antique, with evocations of the Roman Empire. There were painted scenes of significant moments in Charles' life and allusions to the vastness of his domains. No drawings seem to survive, but there are quite detailed descriptions of the *apparati*, and the inscriptions are recorded. Artists known to have worked on the *apparati*: Giorgio Vasari, Il

Tribolo, Ridolfo Ghirlandaio, Cristofano Gherardi, Raffaello da Montelupo, Battista Franco, Fra Giovan Agnolo Montorsoli, Battista Franco, Andrea de' Feltrini, Stefano Veltroni, Baccio d'Agnolo and his son Giuliano, Francesco da San Gallo, Antonio Particini, Tasso (a woodcarver), and Cesare (a sculptor).

Sources

1. LAPINI, *Diario fiorentino*, pp. 99-100.

Some witness information on the emperor's entry and stay.

2. [SALA, ANDREA], *La gloriosa et triumphale entrata di Carlo V. Imp. Aug. in la citta di Firenze, e il significato delli archi triumphali, e statue sopra lor poste, con i loro detti, e versi lattini.* In Sala's *Ordine pompe, apparati,* cc. C4r-D4v.

A careful, systematic account, with recording of inscriptions and much description of *apparati.* Sala is the author of the accounts of the entries into Messina, Naples, Rome, and Siena, but he states that he is here transcribing a letter written by a young Florentine.

3. SANTA CRUZ, *Crónica del Emperador Carlos V,* vol. III, pp. 356-358.

By the emperor's would-be Spanish historiographer, who was probably not present but saw contemporary documents. A rather short account with some description of the *apparati* and several inscriptions in Spanish translation.

4. VANDENESSE, *Journal des voyages de Charles-Quint,* p. 132.

A laconic recording of the emperor's visit by a member of his household.

5. VARCHI, *Storia fiorentina,* tomo II, pp. 214-222.

The author was probably a witness, not yet in exile, but, writing years later, doubtless consulted detailed accounts, including probably those of Sala and Vasari, and he may well have talked with the latter about the entry. He gives information on the procession, considerable description of the *apparati,* and the texts of nearly all the inscriptions mentioned by Vasari (with some small differences of wording).

6. VASARI, in the lives of Raffaello da Montelupo, Il Tribolo, Andrea de' Feltrini, Cristofano Gherardi, Ridolfo Ghirlandaio, Battista Franco, Fra Giovan Agnolo Montorsoli, in the account of his own career, in a letter addressed to Raffael dal Borgo di San Sepolcro dated March 15 (concerned with the preparations), and in another addressed to the writer Pietro Aretino in Venice dated

April 30, *Opere*, vol. IV, p. 545; vol. VI, pp. 67-69, 209-210, 216-217, 545, 573, and 637; vol. VII, 658-659; and vol. VIII, pp. 252-260.

The author was not only one of the principal artists employed in the decorations but also one of the four appointed planners. He gives a great deal of information in the lives of individual artists, and his letter to Aretino is a systematic account, perhaps meant for the eyes of the Venetian government. A major source.

Studies

7. CHASTEL, *Les Entrées de Charles-Quint en Italie*, pp. 202-203.

Using mainly the information given by Vasari, the author describes and comments upon the principal *apparati*, with allusions to those prepared earlier in Rome and Siena.

8. JACQUOT, *Panorama des fêtes et cérémonies du règne*, p. 433.

Analyses the iconography of the *apparati* in the context of that for all the *feste* of Charles' reign.

9. STRONG, *Splendour at Court*, p. 96.

A very short summary of the entry.

VI

1536, May 31-June 13. FESTIVITIES FOR THE MARRIAGE OF DUKE ALESSANDRO DE' MEDICI AND MARGARET OF AUSTRIA, NATURAL DAUGHTER OF THE EMPEROR CHARLES V.

The fourteen-year-old Margaret, who had previously been married to the duke in Naples, entered the city on May 31 by the Porta al Prato, proceeded by Borgo Ognissanti, Canto degli Strozzi, Via Tornabuoni, Canto de' Carnesecchi to the Duomo, then past the Palazzo Medici to the house of Ottaviano de' Medici, where she was first to stay. Relatively little is known of the street decorations, which probably included some left over from the entry of Charles V a month before. A good deal is known of the decorations of Ottaviano de' Medici's house, which included special *apparati* and the display of permanent works of art in the Medici collections. Artists: Giorgio Vasari, Il Tribolo, Battista Franco, Cristofano Gherardi, and Andrea de' Feltrini. June 13: marriage mass in San Lorenzo and the performance in the hall of the Compagnia dei Tessitori, Via San Gallo, of the learned comedy *L'Aridosia* of Lorenzino de' Medici, cousin and soon-to-be assassin of the duke. The special *apparato* for the comedy, one of the first elaborate ones in Florence, included a triumphal arch, a canvas with painted buildings in perspective, and galleries for singers and instrumentalists. Little else is known of the production. There may well have been *intermedii* in verse, written by Lorenzino, with a political or civic content. If so, their disappearance is a grievous loss for political and literary history. The music for the comedy performance is not identified. Artists for the stage setting: Bastiano (Aristotele) da San Gallo and Vasari.

Sources

1. LAPINI, *Diario fiorentino*, p. 100.

A brief account of the entry and wedding festivities.

2. VARCHI, *Storia fiorentina*, tomo II, pp. 222-223.

A short account with some information about the entry. Erroneous statement that the comedy was performed in the Palazzo Medici.

3. VASARI, in the lives of Andrea de' Feltrini, Il Tribolo, Cristofano Gherardi, Bastiano (Aristotele) da San Gallo, and Battista Franco, in a letter to Francesco Rucellai written in May, 1536 (with information about the preparations), and in another addressed to Pietro Aretino in Venice dated June 3. *Opere*, vol. V, p. 210; vol. VI, pp. 69, 217-218, 439-441, and 574; and vol. VIII, pp. 261-265.

Vasari was much involved in the preparations, and he gives a great deal of information. In the life of San Gallo he tells an amazing story of having foiled a plot of Lorenzino de' Medici to have the architect construct part of the *apparato* for the comedy performance in such a way as to make it likely to collapse on the duke's head. His letter to Aretino is a systematic account of the duchess' entry with much information on the decorations of the house of Ottaviano de' Medici. The main source.

Studies

4. D'ANCONA, *Origini del teatro italiano*, vol. II, p. 166.

A short account of the production of the play, with quotations from Vasari and from the ms. diary of Settimanni.

5. *Enciclopedia dello spettacolo*, under « San Gallo », vol. VIII, col. 1477; and under « Vasari », vol. IX, col. 1469.

Summaries of San Gallo's work on the stage setting for the comedy and of Vasari's work on the entry decorations.

6. FABBRI, MARIO, *Il luogo teatrale*, pp. 82-83.

A discussion of the production of *L'Aridosia*, with much bibliographical information, including some references to manuscripts.

7. FACCIOLI, EMILIO, in the introduction to his edition of Lorenzino de' Medici's *Aridosia*, Torino, Einaudi 1974 (« Collezione di teatro », 176), pp. v-viii.

A good summary of what is known of the production, with quotation of Vasari.

8. MANGO, *La commedia in lingua nel Cinquecento*, p. 268.

A description of the first edition of the play, with a summary of its plot and a bibliography.

9. SANESI, *La commedia*, vol. I, pp. 336-339.

An analysis of the play with mention of the circumstances of its first production.

10. ZORZI, *Il teatro e la città*, pp. 88 and 188-189 (note).

A short account of the production of the play and its *apparati*, with bibliographical references.

VII

1539, June 29-July 9. FESTIVITIES FOR THE MARRIAGE OF COSIMO I, DUKE OF FLORENCE, AND ELEONORA DI TOLEDO, DAUGHTER OF THE SPANISH VICEROY OF NAPLES.

The duchess, arriving from Leghorn, entered by the Porta al Prato, proceeded by Borgo Ognissanti, Canto de' Tornaquinci, and Canto de' Carnesecchi to the Duomo, then by Via della Nunziata to Piazza San Marco, then by Via Larga to the Medici Palace. At the Porta al Prato, a triumphal arch by Il Tribolo, with numerous sculptures and painted scenes, and a box holding musicians, who sang a motet *Ingredere* by Francesco Corteccia. At San Marco, an equestrian statue of the duke's father Giovanni delle Bande Nere by Il Tribolo. There were also elaborate decorations, including many paintings, for the entrance and the two courtyards of the Palazzo Medici. Other artists besides Il Tribolo who were employed on various *apparati*: Bastiano (Aristotele) da San Gallo, Agnolo Bronzino, Ridolfo Ghirlandaio, Francesco Salviati, Battista Franco, Francesco Ubertini (Il Bachiacca), Domenico Conti, Pier Francesco di Sandro, Antonio di Domenico, Sandro Buglioni, and Carlo Portelli da Loro. July 6: banquet and pageant in the second courtyard of the palace, with singing and recitation of verses by Apollo and the Muses and by personages representing cities of the duke's domain. *Stanze* and apparently also the verses of the madrigals by Giambattista Gelli, music by Francesco Corteccia, Costanzo Festa, Giovan Pietro Masaconi, and Matteo Rampollini. July 9: performance in the second courtyard of Antonio Landi's learned comedy *Il comodo*, with a stage setting representing Pisa by San Gallo, and seven musical *intermedi* whose verses are by Giovambattista Strozzi the Elder and whose music was composed by Corteccia. Only a few hesitantly identified preparatory drawings for this festival seem to survive (see Kaufmann and Zorzi, below), but there are detailed descriptions and both the verses and the music, as well as the comedy, are preserved. There is rich material for political, literary, musical, and iconographical history.

Sources

1. ANONYMOUS EDITOR, *Musiche fatte nelle nozze dello illustrissimo Duca di Firenze il Signor Cosimo de Medici et della illustrissima consorte sua Mad. Leonora da Tolleto*. Venetia, A. Gardane 1539, 5 part books in 4º oblong. Oestereichische Nationalbibliothek, Vienna.

Includes Corteccia's motet *Ingredere* sung at the Porta al Prato; eight madrigals sung at the banquet, composed by Corteccia, Festa, Masaconi, Moschini, and Rampollini; and seven musical *intermedii* for the comedy, composed by Corteccia.

2. GIAMBULLARI, PIERFRANCESCO, *Apparato et feste nelle noze del Illustrissimo Signor Duca di Firenze, et della Duchessa sua consorte, con le sue stanze, ma-*

driali, comedia, et intermedii in quelle recitate. Fiorenza, Benedetto Giunta 1539, 8°, pp. 176. Biblioteca Nazionale, Florence: Palat. (11).6.9.4.1 IIa.

In the form of a letter to Giovanni Bandini, the duke's ambassador to Charles V, a very full account of the occasion. Narration of the duchess' travel from Naples and her entry into Florence, with detailed description of the *apparati* in the streets and at the Palazzo Medici, and full accounts of the pageant and the production of the comedy. The texts of Gelli's verses for the pageant, Landi's comedy, and Strozzi's verses for the *intermedii* are included, though the music is not and there are no illustrations. This is one of the most informative official accounts of a festival published during the first half of the century. The main source.

3. LANDI, ANTONIO, *Il comodo commedia, con i suoi intermedii recitati nelle nozze del Illustriss. et Eccellentiss. S. il S. Duca di Firenze l'anno 1539.* Fiorenza, Giunti 1566, 8°, pp. 95. Biblioteca Nazionale, Florence: Maglia. 3 G.6250.

A new edition of the comedy with its *intermedii*, probably occasioned by new interest in wedding *feste* after the marriage of the duke's son Francesco in 1565.

4. LANDUCCI, *Diario fiorentino*, p. 375.

In the anonymous continuation, a very brief recording of the duchess' arrival and the festivities.

5. LAPINI, *Diario fiorentino*, pp. 102-103.

A short report of the duchess' entry and the festivities.

6. VASARI, in the lives of Il Tribolo, Bastiano (Aristotele) da San Gallo, Ridolfo Ghirlandaio, Battista Franco, and Francesco Salviati, *Opere*, vol. VI, pp. 86-89, 441-445, 545, and 576-577; and vol. VII, p. 17.

Vasari, though absent from Florence in 1539, knew the artists employed very well, and he gives a great deal of almost first-hand information about all the *apparati*, including the stage setting for the comedy.

Studies

7. ANGELI, UBALDO, *Notizie per la storia del teatro a Firenze nel secolo XVI, specialmente circa gli intermezzi.* Modena, Nahmias 1891, pp. 6-8.

A short discussion of the dramatic skits for the banquet.

8. ANGELI, UBALDO, *La personificazione delle città, paesi e fiumi di Toscana, festeggianti le nozze di Cosimo I ed Eleonora di Toledo tratto da un raro libretto di Pier Francesco Giambullari.* Prato, Tip. Salvi 1898, pp. 30 (Nozze Rostagno-Cavazza).

Reproduces, with background information, Giambullari's account of the banquet and pageant.

9. BORSOOK, EVE, review of the catalogue of the exhibition « Feste ed apparati medicei da Cosimo I a Cosimo III » (Uffizi 1969). « L'Arte Illustrata », no. 27, 1970, p. 137.

Mentions an important ms. source for the wedding festivities.

10. D'ANCONA, *Origini del teatro italiano*, vol. II, p. 166.

Describes the production of *Il comodo*, with quotation of of a passage about it from the ms. diary of Settimanni.

11. *Enciclopedia dello spettacolo*, under « Firenze », vol. V, col. 377.

A good summary of the celebrations.

12. FABBRI, MARIO, *Il luogo teatrale*, pp. 81-82.

A valuable discussion of the banquet pageant and comedy production with quotations from sources and much bibliographical information, including some references to ms. material.

13. GHISI, FEDERICO, *Feste musicali della Firenze medicea (1480-1589)*. Firenze, Vallecchi 1939; repr. Bologna, Forni 1969, pp. xviii-xxii and 49-62.

A learned discussion of the music and musicians for the 1539 *nozze*, with transcription in modern notation of two of Corteccia's *intermedii* for the comedy.

14. GORI, *Firenze magnifica*, pp. 117-124.

A summary of the festivities, poorly documented, with some information on the historical background.

15. KAUFMANN, HENRY, *Art for the Wedding of Cosimo de' Medici and Eleonora of Toledo (1539)*. « Paragone » (Firenze), anno XXI, no. 243, maggio 1970, pp. 52-67 and plates 48a-51.

An excellent study of what is known of the works of art done for the occasion. The author reproduces a drawing of Il Tribolo (Cabinet des Dessins, Louvre) that seems to be a sketch for the equestrian statue of Giovanni delle Bande Nere, and also a number of medallions, ancient coins, and illustrations from emblem books on which many representations of devices and emblems at the Prato Gate and Medici Palace were clearly modelled.

16. KAUFMANN, HENRY, *Music for a Noble Florentine Wedding*, in L. Berman, editor, *Words and Music: The Scholar's View*. Cambridge, Mass. 1972, pp. 271-291.

Not seen. Cited by Pirrotta, below.

17. MANGO, *La commedia in lingua nel Cinquecento*, pp. 114-115.

Describes the first edition of the play, summarizes its plot, and mentions the circumstances of the first production.

18. MINOR, ANDREW, and MITCHELL, BONNER, *A Renaissance Entertainment: Festivities for the Marriage of Cosimo I, Duke of Florence, in 1539*. Columbia, Mo., University of Missouri Press 1968, pp. 373.

An English translation of Giambullari's full text, including the verses and the comedy, and a modern edition of all the music. Introductory chapters on the political, literary, musicological, and art historical background of the *festa*. Numerous notes identifying classical inscriptions on the *apparati* and explaining emblems or historical and mythological allusions.

19. MITCHELL, *Les Intermèdes au service de l'Etat*, pp. 127-129.

A short analysis of the political content of the banquet pageant.

20. NAGLER, ALOIS, *Theatre Festivals of the Medici, 1539-1637*. New Haven, Conn., and London, Yale University Press 1964, pp. 5-12.

A good summary of the festivities, based on Giambullari.

21. PIRROTTA, *Li due Orfei*, pp. 176-187 and 196-199 (notes).

A very good account of the banquet and study of the comedy production with the transcription of the music for five of Corteccia's *intermedii*.

22. POVOLEDO, *Origini e aspetti della scenografia in Italia*, pp. 404-412.

An excellent detailed study of the scenography for the production of the comedy.

23. SANESI, *La commedia*, vol. I, p. 339.

A short analysis of the play with mention of the circumstances of the production.

24. SOLERTI, ANGELO, *Musica, ballo e drammatica alla corte medicea dal 1600 al 1637*. Firenze, Bemporad 1905, pp. 1-3.

A short bibliography for the celebrations with a small amount of commentary.

25. ZORZI, *Il teatro e la città*, pp. 88, 94-96, 193-196 (note), and plates 56 and 57.

The author analyzes in considerable detail the production of *Il comodo*, which he sees as a precedent and prototype for later Medici court productions, gives a number of bibliographical references, and reproduces two drawings, one by Domenico Beccafumi and another by Bastiano da San Gallo, which he considers are relevant to the stage setting. A very valuable study.

VIII

1545, ca. June 23-26. CELEBRATION OF THE FEAST OF SAINT JOHN THE BAPTIST, PATRON SAINT OF THE CITY.

A more elaborate celebration of San Giovanni than had taken place for years, interesting also as a demonstration of the cultural policies of Duke Cosimo I. The Florentine *Potenze* prepared *apparati* that included two triumphal arches along the Arno and other important constructions in the streets. On the eve of San Giovanni there was a parade of *trionfi* prepared by different *compagnie*. These included a triumph of Peace, one of the Liberal Arts, and one of the Trinity. On following days there were a parade of the traditional *carri*, jousts, and bull fights. The duke's secretary Pier Francesco Ricci had an important role in the planning of the celebrations.

Studies

1. BORSOOK, EVE, review of the catalogue of the exhibition « Feste ed apparati medicei da Cosimo I a Cosimo II » (Uffizi 1969). « L'Arte Illustrata », no. 27, 1970, p. 137.

A short description of the festival with the indication of two important ms. sources.

2. PLAISANCE, MICHEL, *La Politique culturelle de Côme 1er et les fêtes annuelles à Florence de 1541 à 1550*. In JACQUOT, *Les Fêtes de la Renaissance III*, pp. 142-145 and 150-151.

A study of the celebrations as an example of Duke Cosimo I's direction of annual festivals for political ends. The author publishes a short ms. description and refers to many other mss.

3. TOSI, C. O., *La festa del San Giovanni nel 1545 a Firenze e le Potenze festeggianti*. « L'Illustratore Fiorentino », calendario storico compilato da Guido Carocci, nuova serie, vol. IV (Firenze, Tip. Domenicana) 1906, pp. 84-92.

A good summary of the celebrations with quotations from ms. sources.

GENOA

I

1502, August 26-ca. September 5. TRIUMPHAL ENTRY AND SOJOURN OF KING LOUIS XII OF FRANCE.

The king, who had received the allegiance of the Genoese republic in Milan in 1499, was paying his first visit to the city. Entry by the Porta San Tommaso, where he was met by the city's *anziani*, elaborate procession under a *baldacchino* to the Duomo of San Lorenzo, which he entered for devotions and for a ceremony of swearing solemnlt to protect the rights of the citizens. He then walked through the Palazzo Ducale, which had been decorated with fleurs-de-lys to receive him, but went to stay instead at the palace of Gian Luigi del Fiesco. Little is known of the *apparati*, which were probably numerous but simple. Decorations with « greenery » and coats of arms are mentioned for the Porta San Tommaso and the portal of the Palazzo Ducale, while the streets of the procession also had greenery and tapestries. Banquets and balls on the days following the entry.

Sources

1. AUTON, JEAN D', *Chroniques*, tome II, pp. 206-221. Main passages printed also in GODEFROY, *Le Cérémonial françois*, tome I, 702-712.

By the king's historiographer, who was present. Much on the procession and costumes, some information also on the simple *apparati*, A main source.

2. FOGLIETTA, *Dell'istorie di Genova*, pp. 581-584 and 595-596. (Pp. 585-594 are omitted in the pagination of the book).

A fairly full account of events with, however, little on the *apparati*.

3. GIUSTINIANI, *Annali della repubblica di Genova*, vol. II, pp. 605-606.

A short summary of events with some information on the city's preparations for receiving the king.

4. PORTO, BENEDETTO DA, *Descriptio adventus Ludovici XII. francorum regis, in urbem Genuam*, authore Benedicto Portuensi, republicae genuensis cancellario. Partly reproduced in GODEFROY, *Le Cérémonial françois*, tome I, pp. 696-701, and wholly in Neri, below.

A systematic account with information about the city's preparations and about the procession, with, however, only vague allusions to the *apparati*. Includes the text of a welcoming oration by the head of the senate.

5. SANUDO, *Diarii*, vol. IV, col. 305.

An undetailed report of the entry.

6. SENAREGA, *De rebus genuensibus commentaria*, pp. 88-90.

A very good contemporary account with some information about the decoration of the palace and much about the procession.

Studies

7. CANALE, *Nuova istoria della repubblica di Genova*, vol. IV, pp. 291-294.

A good summary of events based on the main sources. Publishes a city decree making the day of the entry a permanent holiday.

8. CASONI, *Annali della repubblica di Genova*, p. 22.

A short account of the king's entry and stay.

9. NERI, ACHILLE, ed., *La venuta di Luigi XII a Genova nel MDII descritta da Benedetto da Porto*, nuovamente edita per cura di Achille Neri. « Atti della Società Ligure di Storia Patria », vol. XIII, tomo II, 1880, pp. 907-929.

Publishes the account of Benedetto da Porto, above, providing a great deal of historical information on the author and the occasion.

II

1507, April 28 or 29-ca. May 12. ENTRY AND SOJOURN OF KING LOUIS
XII OF FRANCE.

An extremely dramatic visit by the French king, against whom
the city had rebelled, and whose troops had just crushed the forces
of the rebellion. (A number of leaders of the rebellious party had
fled the city by sea the night before the entry). The king was met
outside the city by a delegation of city fathers dressed in black
asking for mercy. Entry « in arms » by the Porta San Tommaso,
where the king listened unmoved to an oration asking for clemency.
Procession to the Banchi, where the king was met by more Genoese
noblemen, to the Duomo, which the king entered, and where a
choir of 6,000 virgins dressed in white and holding palm branches
sang to implore his mercy. (According to *La Conqueste de Gennes*,
below, ladies were stationed on scaffoldings along the route to beg
for mercy). The king stayed in the Palazzo Ducale. No *apparati*
for the entry. May 11: the king held a « siège royal », or court of
justice, in the courtyard of the Palazzo Ducale, seated on an elaborately decorated platform. Solemn ceremonies in which Genoese
officials prostrated themselves to beg for mercy. Orations were
given on behalf both of the city and of the king, and he burned his
old privileges granted to the city, only to grant it new ones immediately afterward.

Sources

1. ANONYMOUS, *La Conqueste de Gennes, et comment les Francois conqueste-
rent la Bastille, et de la deffense du castellet. Avec lentree du roy en ladicte ville de
Gennes. Et ce qua este fait de par ladicte ville de Gennes pour lentree du roy nostre
dit sire.* Published in CIMBER, *Archives curieuses de l'histoire de France*, tome II,
pp. 13-24.

Apparently a news sheet, perhaps printed in Genoa and then sent back to France.
A careful account of the procession with a reference to platforms in the street from which
well-dressed ladies implored the king for mercy.

2. AUTON, *Chroniques*, tome IV, pp. 4-8, 25-26. The main passages printed also in GODEFROY, *Le Cérémonial françois*, tome I, pp. 712-717.

Perhaps the best account of the entry and of the *siège royal*. Much information on the procession and on the ceremonies in which the Genoese asked the king's pardon.

3. FOGLIETTA, *Dell'istorie di Genova*, pp. 623-628.

A rather full account of the king's entry and stay, including the *siège royal*, from the point of view of the fearful inhabitants.

4. GIUSTINIANI, *Annali della repubblica di Genova*, vol. IV, pp. 631-633.

A short account of events.

5. GUICCIARDINI, *Storia d'Italia*, vol. II, pp. 197-200.

A rather good account of the entry and of the *siège royal*. The author quotes, or paraphrases, the speech of one of the city's *anziani*.

6. MAROT DE CAEN, *Les deux heureux voyages de Genes et Venise*, cc. 22r-23v.

A witness account of the entry, in affected *grand rhétoriqueur* verse, with description of the women in white who implored the king's mercy along the route.

7. PANDOLFINI, FRANCESCO, letter to the Florentine government, dated April 28-May 1, 1507, in DESJARDINS, *Négociations diplomatiques*, tome II, pp. 241-248.

The account of a Florentine ambassador who apparently entered with the king. Much about events immediately preceding and following the entry, some details on the entry itself.

8. SALVAGO, ALESSANDRO, *Cronaca di Genova scritta in francese da Alessandro Salvago*, e pubblicata dal socio Cornelio De Simone. « Atti della Società Ligure di Storia Patria », vol. XIII, fasc. 1, 1884, pp. 479-481.

A short contemporary account of events by a Genoese probably writing for the French governor.

9. SANUDO, *Diarii*, vol. VII, cols. 60-61, 69-70, 72.

Rather laconic accounts of the entry, of events immediately preceding it, and of the king's reception of a Venetian embassy.

10. SENAREGA, *De rebus genuensibus commentaria*, pp. 116-118.

A short witness account of events, including the *siège royal*.

11. CANALE, *Nuova istoria della repubblica di Genova*, vol. IV, pp. 326-333.

A good, detailed summary of the entry and following events.

12. CASONI, *Annali della repubblica di Genova*, pp. 39-42.

A summary of events with the text of Stefano Giustiniani's oration to the king.

13. GODEFROY, *Le Cérémonial françois*, tome I, pp. 712-714.

Has information from an unidentified ms. concerning the procession, the simple decoration of the streets, and the Genoese petitions for mercy.

14. PANDIANI, EMILIO, *Un anno di storia genovese (giugno 1506-1507) con diario e documenti inediti.* « Atti della Società Ligure di Storia Patria », vol. XXXVII, 1905, pp. 716.

The main study of the Genoese revolt and subsequent surrender to the French. The author provides, pp. 268-279, an excellent summary of events during the king's stay, while the anonymous diary gives, pp. 299-410, one of the fullest contemporary accounts.

III

1529, August 12. ENTRY OF THE EMPEROR CHARLES V, ON HIS WAY TO MEET POPE CLEMENT VII IN BOLOGNA.

The emperor arrived by sea, and the Genoese, probably under the orders of Andrea Doria, had built a long special pier out into the water. It was elaborately decorated, and there was apparently a triumphal arch, perhaps where the pier joined the dock, with topical paintings, e.g. one showing the emperor crowning a personage representing the city, and another showing Andrea ruling over the city. A machine in the form of a globe of the world, with an imperial eagle on top, was apparently brought out on to the pier. It opened, scattering scented water, and a young man representing Justice came out and recited verses (not preserved). The emperor entered the city under a *baldacchino*, riding a mule because of the steep hills, and proceeded to the Duomo and the Palazzo della Signoria, where he was to stay.

Sources

1. BONFADIO, *Annali delle cose di Genova*, pp. 49-50.

A short witness account with no attention to *apparati*.

2. GONZAGA, *Cronaca del soggiorno di Carlo V in Italia*, pp. 79-85.

The main source, with a good deal of information about the ceremonies and the *apparati*. The author was probably present.

3. SANTA CRUZ, *Crónica del Emperador Carlos V*, vol. III, p. 66.

A spare report of the emperor's passage through Genoa.

4. VANDENESSE, *Journal des voyages de Charles-Quint*, p. 83.

A spare report of the emperor's arrival.

5. VARCHI, *Storia fiorentina*, vol. II, pp. 23-25.

Includes some specific information about the *apparati* that the author must have obtained at close second hand.

Studies

6. CANALE, *Storia della repubblica di Genova dall'anno 1528 al 1550*, pp. 80-81.

A short account of the emperor's arrival and stay.

7. CASONI, *Annali della repubblica di Genova*, p. 132.

A short account.

8. JACQUOT, *Panorama des fêtes et cérémonies du règne*, p. 441.

A short analysis of the *apparati*.

IV

1548, ca. 26 November-11 December. ENTRY AND VISIT OF PRINCE PHILLIP OF SPAIN, BEGINNING A JOURNEY ACROSS NORTHERN ITALY TOWARD AUSTRIA, GERMANY, AND THE LOW COUNTRIES.

Arrival from Spain by sea with reception by the doge and *signoria* at the port. Climb up the hillside to the Palazzo Doria, where the prince was to stay as guest of Admiral Andrea Doria. Along the way up the hill, a triumphal arch or portico with a dense iconographical content of figures from ancient history, e.g. Publius Scipio, and classical mythology, e.g. Hercules, and inscriptions. The general theme of the *apparato* seems to have been the virtue of princes. In front of the palace there was a machine in the form of a globe of the world which emitted fireworks when the prince (and later important visitors) entered. In order to allow the preparation of further *apparati*, the entry into the city proper was delayed until December 8. The prince then entered by the Porta San Tommaso and proceeded to the Duomo, where he heard a mass with music by the Spanish organist Antonio de Cabeçón. Principal *apparati*: two giants at the Porta San Tommaso; statues of Faith, Liberty, and the god Janus at the Porta della Vacca; a very large triumphal arch at San Ciro, with numerous statues, paintings, and inscriptions glorifying the prince as the worthy son of a great father; smaller arches in the Banchi, in the Piazza di San Giorgio, and in the Piazza di Giustiniano; interior decorations of the Duomo. The identity of artists is not known, and no drawings seem to survive. There are, however, good descriptions, and many inscriptions are recorded.

Sources

1. ALVAREZ, *Relación del camino del Principe de España Don Felipe*, exact reference unknown.

Not seen. Since the author was a member of the prince's party this account may be a major source.

2. ANONYMOUS, *Lettera de l'entrata del Ser. Principe d'Hespagna in Genova*. Place, publisher, and date unknown, 8°, cc. 7. Location unknown.

Not seen. Listed in the anonymous *Catalogue des livres de M. Ruggieri*, p. 144 (item 697). Perhaps an important source.

3. BONFADIO, *Annali delle cose di Genova*, pp. 182-185.

A rather full account of the entry with some description of the *apparati*.

4. CALVETE, *El felicissimo viaje*, cc. 10v-19r.

The main source. Very good descriptions of the *apparati* and the text of many inscriptions.

5. SANTA CRUZ, *Crónica del Emperador Carlos V*, vol. V, pp. 232-241.

A very detailed account with much information on the prince's arrival in Genoa and later official entry. Good descriptions of the *apparati* and recording of inscriptions in Spanish translation. Perhaps derived mainly from Calvete.

6. ULLOA, *Vita e fatti*, cc. 179v-183v.

A good deal of information on the ceremonies and *apparati*, perhaps taken mainly from Calvete, though the author may have been present (as he certainly was at later entries of the prince's journey).

Studies

7. CANALE, *Storia della repubblica di Genova dall'anno 1528 al 1550*, pp. 368-371.

A good deal of information about the circumstances of the prince's visit, and some on the entry itself.

8. CASONI, *Annali della repubblica di Genova*, pp. 191-195.

A good account of events with some attention to *apparati*.

9. JACQUOT, *Panorama des fêtes et cérémonies du règne*, pp. 441-442.

A short analysis of the *apparati*.

10. NICOLINI, *Sul viaggio di Filippo d'Asburgo in Italia*, pp. 213 and 218-233.

A very good summary of events based on all the important sources, including several manuscript ones.

LUCCA

I

1494, 8 November. ENTRY OF KING CHARLES VIII OF FRANCE, ON HIS WAY TO CONQUER THE KINGDOM OF NAPLES.

The king was met outside the city by the officials of the republic and proceeded under a *baldacchino* to the Duomo and the Bishop's Palace, where he stayed overnight. Little is known of the *apparati*, but there is reported to have been a triumphal arch, perhaps simple, and one inscription, welcoming the king as a conquering Caesar, is recorded. There may also have been « mysteries » acted out in the streets at the king's passage.

Sources

1. DESREY, *Relation du voyage du roy Charles VIII*, in Godefroy ed., p. 203; in Cimber ed., p. 219.

A primary source, with mention of « représentations de jeux ».

2. LA VIGNE, *Vergier d'honneur*, ca. 1500 ed., cc. f5v-f6r; *Histoire du voyage de Naples*, p. 117; *La Très Curieuse et Chevaleresque Hystoire de la conqueste de Naples*, pp. 38-39.

A primary source, with mention of the triumphal arch and recording of the inscriptions.

3. SANUDO, *La spedizione di Carlo VIII in Italia*, pp. 109-111.

A little information about the procession, much about the king's reception of ambassadors from other Italian states.

4.   CHERRIER, *Histoire de Charles VIII*, tome II, p. 11.

A short account with little attention to the ceremonies or *apparati*.

5.   DELABORDE, *L'Expédition de Charles VIII en Italie*, p. 446.

A short account of the king's stay with no attention to *apparati*.

II

1536, May 6. ENTRY OF THE EMPEROR CHARLES V DURING HIS TRIUMPHAL PROGRESS UP THE PENINSULA AFTER THE VICTORY OF TUNIS.

Entry by the Porta di Borgo with welcoming ceremonies and then procession under *baldacchino* to the Duomo of San Martino. The emperor then passed from the Duomo to the Bishop's Palace, where he was to stay, by an interior door. Principal *apparati*: at the Porta, the imperial pair of columns with an architrave and frieze bearing the imperial and municipal arms and a welcoming inscription; at Piazza del Palazzo de' Gigli, a large pyramid or « aguglia » with an inscription alluding to Charles' African victories; at the Piazza di San Giovanni, a tall classical column with inscriptions hailing the emperor as the champion of peace and religion; at the door of the Duomo, arms and inscriptions; and inside the Bishop's Palace, decorations and inscriptions. The identity of the artists is not recorded and no sketches seem to have survived, but there is good verbal description and the inscriptions are preserved.

Sources

1.   MONTECATINI, NICOLO, *Entrata dell'imperatore nella citta di Lucca*. N.p., n.d., but probably 1536, 16°, cc. 4. Biblioteca Statale, Lucca: E.V.b.10. Reprinted by Volpi, below.

A formal and systematic account addressed to a high prelate, perhaps the papal nunzio, by a Lucchese gentleman, dated May 10, 1536. Very good descriptions of the procession and *apparati*, with the texts of apparently all the inscriptions. The main source.

2. SANTA CRUZ, *Crónica del Emperador Carlos V*, vol. III, pp. 364-365.

By the emperor's would-be Spanish historiographer, a good account with some description of the *apparati* and Spanish versions of several inscriptions. Perhaps derived mainly from Montecatini.

3. VANDENESSE, *Journal des voyages de Charles-Quint*, p. 132.

A bare recording of the emperor's passage.

Study

4. VOLPI, GIUSEPPE, *Carlo V a Lucca nel MDXXXVI. Lettera di Niccolò Montecatini con note e documenti*. Lucca, Tip. Giusti 1892, pp. 93 (Nozze Pfanner-Morelli).

The author reprints Montecatini's *livret*, above, with a long introduction, copious notes, and a number of relevant documents from the city archives. The notes contain numerous quotations from ms. sources, notably the history of the city by Giuseppe Civitali, which is rich in information. (His wording of the inscriptions sometimes differs from that of Montecatini). The documents include much on the city's preparations and a directive prescribing the ceremonies to be held during the entry.

III

1541, September 8-20. ENTRIES AND SOJOURNS OF POPE PAUL III AND THE EMPEROR CHARLES V.

September 8: solemn entry of the pope, under a *baldacchino*, with procession to the Duomo and the Bishop's Palace, where he stayed. *Apparati* with inscriptions at the city gate, at the Canto d'Arco, at the Canto de' Gigli, at the Duomo, and at the Bishop's Palace. September 12: a simpler entry of the emperor, by the Porta San Donato, without important *apparati*. Procession to the Duomo and to the Palazzo degli Anziani, where Charles stayed. Meetings of the pope and emperor through September 18, date of the latter's departure. Departure of the pope on September 20.

1. « FF. C. », *La entrata della santità di N.S. Papa Paulo III. nella città di Lucca. Colle festi, pompe, e apparati de signori lucchesi. L'aspettatione dell'intrata della Maesta Cesarea, e intendimento della impresa contra infedeli* [...]. Roma, Bal-

dassare Cartolaro Perugino, n.d., 8°, cc. 4. Biblioteca Apostolica Vaticana, Rome: Ferr. V, 9628, int. 7.

The text of a letter written to Ranuccio Farnese from Lucca, between the time of the entry of the pope and that of the arrival of the emperor. A detailed description of the procession for the pope's entry with, however, almost no information on *apparati*.

2. SANTA CRUZ, *Crónica del Emperador Carlos V*, vol. IV, pp. 114-117.

Much information about the discussions of the pope and the emperor, and a little about the procession of the emperor's entry.

3. VANDENESSE, *Journal des voyages de Charles-Quint*, pp. 191-192.

By a member of the emperor's household, a short account of his entry and meetings with the pope.

Studies

4. PASTOR, *Storia dei papi*, vol. V, pp. 433-434.

A short account of the pope's stay in Lucca.

5. SIMONETTI, ADOLFO, *Il convegno di Paolo III e Carlo V in Lucca (1541)*. Lucca, Tip. Alberto Marchi 1901, pp. 55.

A very careful study, based on archival and other ms. material, with some description of the *apparati* and the texts of a number of inscriptions for the pope's entry.

MANTUA

I

1530, March 25–April 19. Entry and Sojourn of Emperor Charles V, en Route to Germany after His Coronation in Bologna.

An elaborate entry and a visit marked by lavish entertainments. Entry by the Portone and Porta della Perdella, procession by the church of San Jacopo and Piazza San Pietro, to the Palazzo Ducale. Principal *apparati*: at the church of San Jacopo, an arch with statues of Habsburg emperors, inscriptions and paintings; at the entrance to Piazza San Pietro, an arch with statues of the goddess Iris (representing War) being put to flight by Mercury (who represents Peace), with inscriptions; in the Piazza San Pietro, a tall wooden column with sixteen paintings showing Charles as master of the world and, on top, a winged statue of Victory in a posture as if she wished to fly down and place a laurel leaf on the head of Charles. On several other days: hunting parties. April 2: visit of the emperor to the Palazzo del Tè, then nearing completion, with a banquet, a ball, and supper. The emperor visited the rooms decorated by Giulio Romano. It is possible one or more comedies were presented during the sovereign's stay (as in 1532), but there is no clear evidence. While in Mantua Charles invested the marquess with the title of duke. The only artist known to have worked on the entry *apparati* (as well as on the permanent decorations of the Palazzo del Tè) is apparently Giulio Romano. The only identified drawing seems to be one he did for the column with the statue of Victory. Some frescoes in the Palazzo del Tè may have been done for the visit or may commemorate it. The inscriptions for the entry *apparati*, though mentioned, are not recorded in published sources.

Sources

1. GIONTA, *Fioretto delle cronache di Mantova*, p. 117.

A brief recording of the emperor's visit.

2. GONZAGA, *Cronaca del soggiorno di Carlo V in Italia*, pp. 239-278.

The main source. The Mantuan author takes pleasure in recounting at length the emperor's activities, and he also gives good descriptions of the *apparati*, though, unfortunately, without recording the inscriptions.

3. SANUDO, *Diarii*, vol. LIII, cols. 78-81, 95-96, and 104-108.

A fair amount of information on the city's preparations, on the entry procession, and on later entertainments.

4. SANTA CRUZ, *Crónica del Emperador Carlos V*, vol. III, p. 93.

A very short account of the emperor's visit.

5. VANDENESSE, *Journal des voyages de Charles-Quint*, p. 94.

A laconic recording of the emperor's passage.

6. VASARI, in the life of Giulio Romano, *Opere*, vol. V, p. 547.

States that Giulio worked on the entry *apparati*, on settings for comedies, and on other things for the emperor's visit. It is not clear, however, whether he is thinking of this visit or of that in 1532.

Studies

7. AMADEI, *Cronaca universale della città di Mantova*, vol. II, pp. 539-541.

A short summary of events during the emperor's stay.

8. CARTWRIGHT, *Isabella d'Este*, vol. II, pp. 323-326.

A good summary of events.

9. CHASTEL, *Les Entrées italiennes de Charles-Quint*, pp. 198-199.

A short study of the *apparati*.

10. CONIGLIO, GIUSEPPE, *I Gonzaga*. [Milano], Dall'Oglio 1967, pp. 274-277.

A general account of events based on the chronicle of Luigi Gonzaga, above.

11. FACCIOLI, *Mantova: le lettere*, vol. II, pp. 252-254 and 270-271.

A short account with a quoted passage from Gonzaga's *Cronaca*.

12. HARTT, *Giulio Romano*, vol. I, pp. 105-106, 148-150, 157-158 and 269-271; vol. II, fig. 523.

Discusses Charles V's visit to the Palazzo del Tè, suggests that some of its decorations may have been done for this visit or that in 1532, and reproduces the drawing for the column with a statue of Victory.

13. JACQUOT, *Panorama des fêtes et cérémonies du règne*, pp. 426-427.

A good short analysis of the *apparati* for the entry.

14. LUZIO, ALESSANDRO, *Isabella d'Este e il sacco di Roma*. « Archivio Storico Lombardo », anno XXXV, serie 4ª, vol. X, 1908, p. 105.

Quotes a letter of Isabella d'Este to her son Ercole, dated April 27, 1530, about the emperor's stay in Mantua, and particularly about three visits he paid to her.

15. MARANI, ERCOLE, and PERINA, CHIARA, *Mantova: le arti*, vol. II. Mantova, Istituto Carlo d'Arco per la Storia di Mantova 1961, pp. 449-450, 452, 455-456, and 486-487.

States that the decorations of the Sala degli Stucchi in the Palazzo del Tè were inspired by the 1530 visit of the emperor and suggests that the Sala di Cesare and the Sala dei Giganti also allude to this visit or to that of 1532.

16. MAZZOLDI, *Mantova: la storia*, vol. II, pp. 301, 360, and 504-506.

A short account of the occasion, with reference to some ms. sources, and a long quotation from Gonzaga's narrative.

17. POSSEVINO, *Gonzaga*, p. 728.

A short, undetailed account.

II

1532, ca. November 7-29. VISIT OF THE EMPEROR CHARLES V, COMING FROM GERMANY TO MEET POPE PAUL III IN BOLOGNA.

It is not sure that there was a grand entry with *apparati*, but comedies, perhaps including *La calandria* of Bernardo Dovizi da Bibbiena, seem to have been given for the emperor's entertainment. During his stay he crowned the poet Ludovico Ariosto with the laurel leaf.

Sources

1.   GIONTA, *Fioretto delle cronache di Mantova*, pp. 117-118.

A short account, with mention of Ariosto's coronation.

2.   SANTA CRUZ, *Crónica del Emperador Carlos V*, vol. III, p. 142.

A very short general account.

3.   VANDENESSE, *Journal des voyages de Charles-Quint*, p. 105.

A bare recording of the emperor's visit.

4.   VASARI, in the life of Giulio Romano, *Opere*, vol. V, p. 547.

States that Giulio worked on the entry *apparati*, on the settings for comedies, and on other things for a visit of the emperor to Mantua. It is not clear whether he means this entry or that of 1530.

Studies

5.   AMADEI, *Cronaca universale della città di Mantova*, vol. II, pp. 546-547.

A short account with mention of Ariosto's coronation.

6.   D'ANCONA, *Origini del teatro italiano*, vol. II, p. 431.

Quotes a letter of the duke asking Filippo Zocco to come and put on comedies, Vasari's remarks about Giulio Romano's participation, and a letter of the court official Calandra complaining about Giulio's work on the stage setting.

7.   *Enciclopedia dello spettacolo*, under « Giulio Romano », vol. V, cols. 1350-1351, and under « Mantova », vol. VII, cols. 67-68.

Discusses what is known of the production of the comedies, with quotation of a document from the Gonzaga archives.

8.   FACCIOLI, *Mantova: le lettere*, vol. II, pp. 254-256, and 271.

Discusses the preparations for the staging of comedies, with speculation that one may have been Bibbiena's *La calandria*, and reproduces Calandra's letter complaining of Giulio Romano's work on the stage settings.

9. HARTT, *Giulio Romano*, vol. I, pp. 271-273 and 356-357.

Discusses Romano's work in connection with the visit and reproduces the complaining letter of Calandra.

10. MAZZOLDI, *Mantova: la storia*, vol. II, p. 303.

A short report of the visit with reference to one ms. source.

III

1549, January 13-17. ENTRY AND SOJOURN OF PRINCE PHILLIP OF SPAIN, ON HIS WAY TO GERMANY AND THE LOW COUNTRIES.

Entry by the Porta della Perdella, elaborate procession to the Duomo and the Palazzo Ducale. The *apparati* included three triumphal arches, one of which had statues of Vergil (Mantuan by birth) and of Ocno, legendary founder of the city, and the others representations of mythological figures (e.g. Argos, Mercury, and Janus) and personified virtues. At the Piazza del Duomo there was a statue of an Hilaritas Publica, and in the Piazza del Castello a statue of Hercules. At the entrance to the palace was a painting of the emperor's conferral of the title of duke on the ruler of the city in 1530. On later days there were hunting parties and, perhaps, one or more performances of comedies. No drawings of the entry *apparati* seem to have survived. It is quite possible that Giovan Battista Bertani, successor to Giulio Romano in the duke's service, may have worked of them. A number of inscriptions are recorded.

Sources

1. ALVAREZ, *Relación del camino del Principe de España Don Felipe*, exact reference unknown.

Not seen. Since the author was a member of the prince's party it is possible that his account may be an important source.

2. ANONYMOUS, *Descrittione delli archi et dechiaratione delle statove, e apparati publici, fatti alla entrata in Mantova del serenissimo prencipe di Spagna, a xiii di gennaro. M.D.XLIX. Con l'accoglienza fatta da Sua Altezza all'illustriss. S. Duca di Ferrara, et l'honore fattoli dalli signori venetiani a Villafranca.* N.p., n.d., but doubtless 1549, 4°, cc. 4. British Museum, London: 9930 bbb. 42.

Apparently a private letter, perhaps addressed to a correspondent in Venice. Very careful descriptions of the entry *apparati*, which the author says were done in eight to ten days. The texts of numerous Latin inscriptions. Much information also on the procession, including costumes. A major source.

3. CALVETE, *El felicissimo viaje,* cc. 36v-40v.

By a member of the prince's party, good descriptions of the *apparati* with the text of some inscriptions. Some information as well on later entertainments. A major source.

4. GIONTA, *Fioretto delle cronache di Mantova,* p. 124.

A short recording of the prince's visit.

5. SANTA CRUZ, *Crónica del Emperador Carlos V,* vol. V, pp. 258-263.

A detailed account of the prince's entry, with description of the *apparati* and Spanish translations of inscriptions. Some information as well on later entertainments. The author states that there were « muchas comedias », but he may well be using the term loosely. His information is perhaps derived mainly from Calvete.

6. ULLOA, *Vita e fatti dell'invitissimo imperatore Carlo V,* cc. 186v-187v.

A short account with, however, some description of the *apparati* and some inscriptions. It is quite possible that the author was present, though he has probably used Calvete's account to refresh his memory.

Studies

7. AMADEI, *Cronaca universale della città di Mantova,* vol. II, pp. 642-645.

A short account that the author has taken mainly from Ulloa.

8. FABBRI, *Gusto scenico a Mantova,* pp. 9-11.

Quotes from Ulloa's account and suggests, later, that Giovan Battista Bertani may have worked on the *apparati.*

9. JACQUOT, *Panorama des fêtes et cérémonies du règne,* p. 444.

A short analysis of the *apparati.*

10. Mazzoldi, *Mantova: la storia*, vol. II, pp. 318 and 372.

Short accounts based on Amadei and Ulloa.

11. Nicolini, *Sul viaggio di Filippo d'Asburgo in Italia*, pp. 260-262.

A summary of events based on numerous sources, including several ms. ones. Some descriptions of *apparati*.

IV

1549, October 22 and following days. Entry of Caterina d'Austria, Bride of Duke Francesco Gonzaga, and Following Entertainments.

A solemn entry with triumphal arches. On October 23, a wedding service in the church of Sant'Andrea read by the poet Girolamo Vida. Several days of entertainments including jousts, a naumachia, and the playing of comedies (whose titles seem to be unknown).

Sources

1. Anonymous, *L'entrata della serenissima et illustrissima signora Caterina d'Austria sposa dell'eccellentissimo duca di Mantova et marchese di Monferrato nella detta sua città*. Mantova, Jacomo Ruffinelli 1549. Location unknown.

Not seen. Quoted by Fabbri, below, and mentioned also by Faccioli, below. Doubtless the main source.

2. Gionta, *Fioretto delle cronache di Mantova*, p. 124.

A short account of Caterina's arrival and marriage.

Studies

3. Amadei, *Cronaca universale della città di Mantova*, vol. II, pp. 648-649.

A short, general account.

4. D'Ancona, *Origini del teatro italiano*, vol. II, pp. 401-402 and 441.

An account of preparations for the staging of the comedies, with quotations from a ms. letter.

5. FABBRI, *Gusto scenico a Mantova*, pp. 29-30.

Quotes from the anonymous *Entrata*, above, a passage about a failure in the execution of the naumachia.

6. FACCIOLI, *Mantova: le lettere*, vol. II, pp. 567-568 and 603.

Some information on the entry and entertainments, from the anonymous *Entrata*, above, and quotation of one of Sabino Calandra's letters about the preparations for the comedies.

7. INTRA, G. B., *Nozze e funerali alla corte dei Gonzaga, 1549-1550*. « Archivio Storico Lombardo », serie 3ª, anno XXIII, 1896, pp. 381-410.

A great deal of information on the historical background of the marriage and on the preparations for the festivities. Long quotations from ms. letters of Sabino Calandra, who was in charge, to his patron Ferrante Gonzaga and others. Particularly interesting are details about the preparations for the playing of the (unidentified) comedies in the Palazzo della Ragione. The author has as well a short account of the entry.

MESSINA

I

1535, October 21. ENTRY OF THE EMPEROR CHARLES V, BEGINNING A TRIUMPHAL PROGRESS THROUGH ITALY AFTER THE VICTORY OF TUNIS.

An elaborate entry with very interesting *apparati*, including some complicated « machines ». As the emperor approached the Porta di Sant'Antonio he passed three arches of greenery representing Concord, Peace, and Victory. He was met by nobles and clergy of the city (including some clergy of the Greek rite or of the Greek Orthodox Church). Just outside the walls, there was a triumphal arch with winged Victories and figures of saints. Outside the Gate there came at least two triumphal chariots, one of them loaded with spoils and pulled by Moors, and another with the four Cardinal Virtues. There was also a globe of the world topped by a statue of the emperor, perhaps on a third chariot or perhaps on one of the foregoing. At the Piazza del Duomo there were two specially decorated fountains. The facade of the Duomo had the pair of imperial columns, topped by genuine ancient sculpted heads representing Scipio Africanus Major and Hannibal, and a machine by which angels descended to take trophies from one of the carts (which had preceded Charles in the procession) and carry them back up to « Heaven ». There was also a triumphal arch in front of the palace where the emperor stayed. Nearly all these *apparati* had inscriptions, which are recorded. On the following Sunday, as the emperor attended mass in the Duomo, there was a machine suspended from the ceiling representing the city of Constantinople. An imperial eagle came to set it on fire with rockets, and a Turkish flag flying over the city was seen to be lowered. Artist known to have been in charge of the preparation of the *apparati*: Polidoro da Caravaggio. Some of his drawings survive (see Strong, below).

Sources

1. ALIBRANDO, COLA GIACOMO D', *Il triumpho il qual fece Messina nella intrata del Imperator Carlo V* [...]. Messina, Pieruccio Spira 1535, 4°. Location unknown.

Not seen. Cited by Castaldo and the anonymous author of the *Memorie de' pittori messinesi*, both below. Doubtless an important source.

2. ANONYMOUS, *Relation de l'entrée de Charles-Quint dans la ville de Messine: 20 octobre 1536*. In GACHARD, *Collection des voyages des souverains des Pays-Bas*, tome II, pp. 567-572.

By a French-speaking soldier in the service of Charles V, a naïve but detailed description of the *apparati*, with the inscriptions given in French translation. There is a particularly enthusiastic account of the machine in the Duomo that depicted a capture of Constantinople.

3. MONTOICHE, *Voyage et expédition de Charles-Quint*, pp. 381-382.

Probably by a soldier in the service of the emperor, a short account with some mention of the *apparati*.

4. [SALA, ANDREA], *La triomphale intrata della Cesarea Maesta in la nobile citta di Messina, con tutti i loro progressi*. In Sala's *La triomphale entrata di Carlo. V. Imperatore Augusto in la inclita citta di Napoli e Missina*, cc. B4r-C4v. Also published separately as *Copia di una lettera della particularita dell'ordine con il quale la Maesta Cesarea intro in Messina, e del triumpho et sumptuosi apparati gli furono fatti* [...]. N.p., n.d., probably 1535, 4°. British Museum, London: 9930 c 4.

A careful and systematic account with good descriptions of the *apparati* and recording of the inscriptions. Done by the man who was soon to describe as well the entries into Naples, Rome, Siena, and Florence. The main source.

5. SANTA CRUZ, *Crónica del Emperador Carlos Quintos*, vol. III, pp. 294-301.

By a contemporary Spanish biographer of the emperor, quite a detailed account with considerable description of the *apparati* and explanation of their mythological and historical allusions. Some inscriptions in Spanish translation. The author was probably not present but must have used detailed contemporary documents.

6. VASARI, in the life of Polidoro da Caravaggio, *Opere*, vol. V, p. 151.

Interesting information about Polidoro's work on the *apparati*.

Studies

7. ANONYMOUS, *Memorie de' pittori messinesi e degli esteri che in Messina fiorirono dal secolo XII, sino al secolo XIX*. Messina, Giuseppe Pappalardo 1821, pp. 42-43. Anastatic reprint, Bologna, Forni 1972.

A study of Polidoro's work on the *apparati*, based mainly on the account of Alibrando, listed above. Conjectures that Polidoro did the two main arches himself and directed his students in the other work.

8. CASTALDO, V., *Il viaggio di Carlo V in Sicilia (1535) secondo una cronaca manoscritta napoletana*. « Archivio Storico per la Sicilia Orientale », serie 2ª, anno V, vol. XXV, 1929, pp. 98-106.

The author quotes some passages and summarizes others from a anonymous Neapolitan chronicle, perhaps by Antonio G. Tommaso and Carlo Mercadanti, that contains a good amount of information about the entry, including description of the *apparati* and the texts of inscriptions. The information may be derived from Alibrando and Sala, above. The author of the study also supplies information of his own, particularly concerning political negotiations during the emperor's stay.

9. JACQUOT, *Panorama des fêtes et cérémonies du règne*, pp. 429-430.

An excellent short analysis of the *apparati*.

10. STRONG, *Splendour at Court*, pp. 93-94 and figs. 72-73.

A good short study of the entry with reproduction of two of Polidoro's preparatory drawings.

MILAN

I

1495, May 26. Investiture of Ludovico Sforza, « il Moro », as Duke of Milan, after the Death of Duke Gian Galeazzo and the Formation of the League against Charles VIII of France.

Very elaborate ceremonies in the Piazza del Duomo, with investiture by an imperial ambassador, after a procession from the Castello that included Milanese officials, ambassadors from other states, and noble ladies in decorated chariots. Main *apparati*: horns of plenty in the streets; at the entrance to the Piazza, a sort of triumphal arch with painting (undescribed); and in the Piazza, an enormous decorated platform with loggias for honored guests and an altar displaying many precious holy vessels.

Sources

1. Cagnola, *Storia di Milano*, p. 196.

A short account with general references to the *apparato* in the Piazza del Duomo.

2. Sanudo, *La spedizione di Carlo VIII in Italia*, pp. 353-355.

A detailed account that is the source of nearly all our knowledge of the occasion.

Studies

3. Dina, Achille, *Isabella d'Aragona duchessa di Milano e Bari*. « Archivio Storico Lombardo », serie 5ª, anno XLVIII, 1921, p. 365.

A summary of the ceremonies.

4. SEGRE, ARTURO, *I prodromi della ritirata di Carlo VIII, re di Francia, da Napoli.* «Archivio Storico Italiano», vol. XXXIV, 1904, pp. 385-387.

Publishes from the Venetian Archivio di Stato a ms. letter addressed to the Doge by four Venetians present in Milan. It contains a good description of the platform erected for the investiture.

II

1499, October 6-Novembre 7. ENTRY AND SOJOURN OF KING LOUIS XII OF FRANCE, WHO HAS JUST CONQUERED THE CITY.

A triumphal entry with the king wearing ducal mantle and beret, his *baldacchino* carried by doctors of the city, from Sant'Eustorgio by the Porta Ticinese to the Duomo and the Castello, with an elaborate procession. Relatively little information on the probably simple *apparati*. A figure of Saint Ambrose at the Porta, tapestries and coats of arms along the streets, and two arches (not described). Several ruling princes and ambassadors from all the Italian powers, prominent among them his allies the Venetians, had gathered to meet the king in Milan. Several banquets and other entertainments during his stay.

Sources

1. ANONYMOUS, *Ingressus Xp̄ianissimi Ludovici francorum regis in civitatem suam mediolaneñ.* N.p., 1499, 4°, cc. 4. British Museum, London: I A. 19043.

Not seen.

2. AUTON, *Chroniques*, tome I, pp. 56-61.

An account by the king's historian, who was present. Much on the procession, little on the *apparati*, some information on later entertainments during the king's stay.

3. CASTIGLIONE, BALDASSARRE, *Lettere del Conte Baldassarre Castiglione*, ora per la prima volta date in luce [...] dall'Abate Pier Antonio Serassi. Padova, Giuseppe Comino 1769, vol. I, pp. 3-5.

A letter to the writer's brother-in-law dated from Milan October 8, 1499. Castiglione, who had come to the city with his patron the marquess of Mantua to meet the king, gives a good account of the procession, with, however, only general allusions to the *apparati*.

4. PAULLO, *Cronaca milanese*, p. 126.

The author does not describe the entry, having been away in Asti, but his editor publishes a city decree ordering the citizens to clean and decorate the route of the procession.

5. PRATO, *Storia di Milano*, pp. 227-230 and 235.

Much information on the procession and the costumes, little on the *apparati*.

6. PRIULI, *Diarii*, vol. I, pp. 204 and 208-209.

A rather full account of the entry, from the point of view of Venetian ambassadors. Only vague references to the *apparati*.

7. SANUDO, *Diarii*, vol. III, cols. 24-26.

An account from a Venetian ambassador, with additional details from the compiler. Much on the procession, little on the triumphal *apparati*. Sanudo records, however, an unofficial *apparato* erected by some Milanese angry at the Venetians for having helped the French. The construction, which depicted a Saint Mark fleeing from the land back out to sea, was demolished by a Venetian nobleman.

Studies

8. PÉLISSIER, LÉON-G., *Les Préparatifs de l'entrée de Louis XII à Milan, d'après les documents des archives italiennes avec les preuves*. Montpellier, Gustave Firmin et Montane, 1891, pp. 55 (Mariage Lefranc-Vauthier).

A detailed study of the Milanese preparations for the king's entry, with the publication of several ms. letters and other documents. Little on the entry itself.

9. TRECCANI, *Storia di Milano*, vol. VII, pp. 504-505.

A very short account of the king's arrival and stay.

III

1507, May 24 to mid-June. ENTRY AND SOJOURN OF KING LOUIS XII OF FRANCE AFTER THE RECONQUEST OF GENOA.

An elaborate triumphal entry with classical themes. The king entered by the Porta Ticinese and proceeded to the Duomo and then to the Castello. Two triumphal chariots, one with real trophies of war and the other with characters representing the four Cardinal Virtues and a Victory, one of whom spoke verses to the king. Three triumphal arches: one outside the gate at Sant'Eustorgio, with, apparently, a figure of Saint Ambrose; another at the Porta; and a third at the Contrada delle Bandiere, with characters representing Italian cities, Italy herself, a Mars and a Jove, the last of whom spoke verses to the king on his passage. No drawings or other works of art from the entry seem to survive, and the artists are apparently not known. Some inscriptions and verses recited before the king are, however, recorded. There were numerous banquets during the king's stay, and on June 14 there was an elaborate joust in the Piazza del Castello.

Sources

1. AUTON, *Chroniques*, tome IV, pp. 60-105. The most relevant passages reprinted in GODEFROY, *Le Cérémonial françois*, tome I, pp. 721-729.

By the king's historiographer, who was present, a very good account of the entry, with description of the *apparati* and some recording of inscriptions. Much information as well about the planning of the tournament and about several banquets given during the king's stay.

2. MAROT DE CAEN, *Les Deux Heureux Voyages de Genes et Venise*, cc. 24r-25r.

An affected witness account of the king's entry, in *grand rhétoriqueur* verse, with mention of a triumphal chariot and of an *apparato* near the city gate on which was depicted the king's victory over the Genoese.

3. PAULLO, *Cronaca milanese*, pp. 193-204 and 374-376.

A careful witness account of the entry with a great deal of information about the *apparati* (sometimes with the names of the citizens who commissioned them) and the recording of numerous inscriptions. Information as well on the *apparati* at a banquet given to the king by his Milanese ally Trivulzio on May 30. The editor publishes, pp. 374-376, a decree ordering the Milanese to prepare the route of the king's entry.

4. PÉLISSIER, LÉON-G., ed., *Documents pour l'histoire de la domination française dans le Milanais (1499-1513)*. Toulouse, Privat 1891 (« Bibliothèque Méridionale », 2e série, I), p. 157.

Publishes a decree of the city government ordering the citizens to clean up the streets and decorate them with « archi triunfali di argenterie, fiori ed altre gentilezze ».

5. Prato, *Storia di Milano*, pp. 260-264.

An enthusiastic and full account by an apparently pro-French Milanese patrician. Much information about the procession and *apparati* for the entry, with some recording of the Italian verses recited by the characters on the *apparati*. Information as well about the joust and about banquets given on later days. In the account of one of the banquets the author gives the text of a peculiar sonnet partly in Italian and partly in Latin that was sung before the king. A major source.

6. Sanudo, *Diarii*, vol. VII, cols. 83-84 and 89-93.

Quite full accounts of the entry from the Venetian ambassadors and from Andrea Magno of Cremona. That of the latter is particularly systematic. Good reports of the entry procession, much description of the *apparati*, some Latin inscriptions, and the text of 32 *endecasillabo* verses recited to the king. A major source.

Studies

7. Chartrou, *Les Entrées solennelles et triomphales à la Renaissance*, p. 76.

A short summary of the entry, based on D'Auton and Marot de Caen.

8. Luzio, Alessandro, *Isabella d'Este e la corte sforzesca*. « Archivio Storico Lombardo », anno XXVIII, serie 3ª, vol. XV, 1901, pp. 157-159.

In telling of Isabella d'Este's visit to Milan during the king's stay, the author quotes a letter she had written to her sister-in-law the duchess of Urbino with information on the joust and other entertainments.

9. D'Ancona, *Origini del teatro italiano*, vol. I, pp. 225-227 (notes).

Reports Prato's account of the recitation at the third arch and gives four of the verses.

10. Treccani, *Storia di Milano*, vol. VIII, pp. 101-102.

A summary of the entry with some description of the *apparati*.

IV

1509, July 1. Triumphal Return to the City of King Louis XII of France, after a Victorious Campaign against the Republic of Venice.

The king had made a simple entry into the city on May 1, just after arriving in Italy from France. On July 1 he returned after some victorious battles in which he had taken several cities from the Venetians. The entry was very elaborate, though there had not been time to finish the *apparati*. The king entered by the Porta Romana. There were four (unfinished) triumphal arches: one outside the gate, one at the gate, one at the door of the Duomo, and a final one, the largest, in the Piazza del Castello. The last had an equestrian statue of the king and (presumably painted) scenes of his battles. There was also a dramatic skit in which personages representing five conquered cities were brought before the king. He was invited to mount into a triumphal chariot drawn by four white horses but declined to do so. The descriptions of the *apparati* are not in general very full. Some inscriptions are recorded. The names of artists are not recorded. Since Leonardo da Vinci was working in the city at this time, in the employment of the French governor, it does not seem unlikely that he may have worked on the *apparati*.

Sources

1. ANONYMOUS, *Oeuvre nouvellement translatée de rime italiene en rime francoyse contenant l'avenement du tres chrestien Loys XII de ce nom a Millan, et sa triumphante entree au dit Millan* [...]. Lyon, 1509, 4°.

Not seen. Listed by CHARTROU, *Les Entrées solennelles et triomphantes à la Renaissance*, in the bibliography at the end of the volume.

2. MAROT DE CAEN, *Les Deux Heureux Voyages de Genes et Venise*, cc. 123r-132v.

Quite a full account of the entry, in affected *grand rhétoriqueur* verse, with considerable description of the chariot and other *apparati*. Some information as well about later events during the king's stay. An important source.

3. FLORANGE, *Mémoires*, tome I, pp. 40-42.

The author's account is not very detailed, but his editors quote some ms. letters of envoys from other cities that contain some information on the *apparati*.

4. PAULLO, *Cronaca milanese*, pp. 251-252.

A short account of the entry, erroneously dated by the author as June 13, with some description of the triumphal chariot, which he says was taken afterward to the Duomo.

5. PRATO, *Storia di Milano*, p. 277.

A short account of the entry with, however, a good deal of information on the *apparati*. An important source.

6. PRIULI, *Diarii*, vol. IV, pp. 117 and 122-123.

A good amount of information apparently derived mainly from letters received by Milanese living in Venice. The editors note other sources.

7. SANUDO, *Diarii*, vol. VIII, col. 478.

The Venetians were less well informed on this entry than on others because they were at war with France, but Sanudo prints the report of an « explorator » who was present. Considerable description of the triumphal chariot.

Study

8. CHARTROU, *Les Entrées solennelles et triomphales à la Renaissance*, pp. 76-77.

A good summary of the entry, based on Florange and Marot de Caen. The author suggests that Leonardo da Vinci may have been in charge of preparing the *apparati*.

V

1512, December 29. A TRIUMPHAL ENTRY OF DUKE MASSIMILIANO SFORZA AFTER THE EXPULSION OF THE FRENCH FROM THE CITY.

A rather elaborate entry by the Porta Ticinese with solemn procession to the Duomo and the palace on the Piazza called the Corte. At least three important *apparati*: one at the Porta with an inscription welcoming the duke; a triumphal arch at the Contrada delle Bandiere with inscriptions and characters representing the four Cardinal Virtues and Fortune, the last of whom recited verses to the duke; and a decoration with inscriptions at the Duomo. There are fairly good descriptions of the *apparati*, and the verses and several inscriptions are recorded. The identity of the artists does not seem to be known.

Sources

1. Burigozzo, *Cronica milanese*, p. 423.

A short account with simple references to some of the *apparati*.

2. Guicciardini, *Storia d'Italia*, vol. III, pp. 242-243.

Some information on the entry, including a dramatic dispute over precedence.

3. Paullo, *Cronaca milanese*, pp. 288-294.

A very good account of the entry with some description of the *apparati*, the texts of a number of inscriptions, and that of some hundred verses in *terza rima* written to be recited before the duke. (He heard only about half of them before becoming impatient and moving on).

4. Prato, *Storia di Milano*, pp. 304-307.

An informative account with a good deal of description of the *apparati* and the text of some inscriptions. For the verses recited to the duke, however, the author has substituted others of his own composition, finding the original ones to be « un poco domestici », that is, rather unpolished.

5. Sanudo, *Diarii*, vol. XV, cols. 456 and 458-460.

Much information on the ceremonies and procession, nothing on the *apparati*.

Study

6. Treccani, *Storia di Milano*, vol. VIII, p. 132.

A summary of the entry with some information on the *apparati* and the text of an inscription.

VI

1515, October 11-ca. October 28. Entry and Sojourn of King Francis I of France, After Regaining the Duchy of Milan by His Victory at Marignan.

The king entered « in arms » but under a *baldacchino* by the Porta Ticinese and proceeded solemnly to the Duomo and then to the palace of the Corte, where he was to stay. There were ceremonies of welcome, but the *apparati* in the streets, little described in the sources, were apparently simple. In the Duomo, suspended from the ceiling, was a machine with a Virgin and Child and a personage representing Milan, with an inscription extolling the virtue of clemency. Jousts before the Castello a week after the entry.

Sources

1. ANONYMOUS, *L'Ordonnance faicte a lentree du treschrétien roy de France Francoys de Valoys premier de ce nom dedans la ville de Millan; le xvi jour doctobre. mil. V cens et. xv. Avec la chanson et salutacion et baterie du chasteau de Millan.* N.p., but probably Milan or Paris, n. pub., 1515, 8°, cc. 4. Bibliothèque Nationale, Paris: Rés. Lb.³⁰. 28.

A good deal of information on the procession but nothing on the *apparati*. The second part of the *plaquette* is given to a satirical « Chanson des Suisses » inspired by Francis' victory at Marignan.

2. BARRILLON, *Journal*, vol. I, pp. 160-162.

A short witness account of the king's entry and stay, with only general allusions to the entry *apparati*.

3. BUGATI, *Historia universale*, p. 747.

A short account with some mention of the jousts and other entertainments.

4. BURIGOZZO, *Cronica milanese*, p. 429.

Some information on the procession with passing mention of the *apparati*.

5. FLORANGE, *Mémoires*, tome I, pp. 207-209. Reprinted in GODEFROY, *Le Cérémonial françois*, tome I, pp. 751-752.

A short witness account of the procession and of later entertainments.

6. LE MOYNE, PASQUIER, *Le Couronnement du Roy Francois premier de ce nom, voyage et conqueste de la [sic] duché de Millan, victoire et repulsion des exurpateurs dicelle [...] fais lan mil cinq cens et quinze, cueillies et rediges par le moyne sans froc.* Paris, Gillet Couteau 1520, 8°, cc. n8v-o2v. Bibliothèque Nationale, Paris: Rés. Lb³⁰. 23.

The author is rather laconic in his description of *apparati* in the streets, but that or the « machine » suspended in the Duomo is highly detailed and of great interest. An important source.

7. PRATO, *Storia di Milano*, p. 347.

A short account with some information on the ceremonies and the procession.

8. SANUDO, *Diarii*, vol. XXI, cols. 233-234, 236-238, and 291-303.

Several letters describing the procession, costumes, and (cols. 291-303) the king's reception of the Venetian ambassadors.

Studies

9. BELTRAMI, LUCA, *Notizie sconosciute sulle città di Pavia e Milano al principio del secolo XVI.* « Archivio Storico Lombardo », serie seconda, anno XVII, 1890, pp. 408-428.

Much information on the historical background of the entry and the quotation, pp. 416-419, of passages from the diary of Le Moyne, above. The latter contain some information on the *apparati* (which the author calls « joyeusetés »), particularly on that in the Duomo.

10. STEFANI, FEDERICO, ed., *Entrata solenne e soggiorno in Milano dell'ambasciata veneta al Cristianissimo Re Francesco I (novembre, 1515).* Venezia, Tip. Antonelli 1870, pp. 24 (Nozze Brambilla-Besana).

The editor brings together the letters of Sanudo's *Diarii* (then still unpublished but noted above) concerning the arrival in Milan of the embassy from Venice, an ally of France, their meeting with the king, and several later banquets. He provides a brief historical introduction and a number of explanatory notes.

11. TRECCANI, *Storia di Milano*, vol. VIII, pp. 190-191.

A short account of the entry, with reference to the description of Le Moyne, above.

VII

1534, May 3. ENTRY OF CHRISTINE OF DENMARK, NIECE OF THE EMPEROR CHARLES V AND NEW BRIDE OF DUKE FRANCESCO II SFORZA.

Entry by the Porta Ticinese and procession to the Duomo and Castello. Main *apparati*: arches at the Ponte di Sant'Eustorgio, the Porta Ticinese, and « al Dazio », and decorations both inside and outside the Duomo. Those inside the church included wooden statues of Saints Ambrose, Protasius, and Gervasius. Some inscriptions are recorded.

Sources

1. BUGATI, *Historia universale*, pp. 819-820.

A short account with some details by a probable witness.

2. BURIGOZZO, *Cronica milanese*, pp. 517-520.

Quite a good account of the entry with some description of the *apparati* and the text of some inscriptions. The main source.

Study

3. TRECCANI, *Storia di Milano*, vol. VIII, pp. 327-330, and vol. X, pp. 917-918.

Two discussions of the new duchess' arrival with, in the second, long quotations of Burigozzo, above.

VIII

1541, August 22-29. ENTRY AND SOJOURN OF THE EMPEROR CHARLES V, COMING FROM GERMANY ON HIS WAY TO MEET POPE PAUL III IN LUCCA, AND THEN TO LEAD AN EXPEDITION TO NORTH AFRICA.

A solemn triumphal entry, by the Porta Romana, past the Contrada degli Aurefici to the Duomo and Corte, with a very elaborate procession. Five triumphal arches: one outside the gate with statues of the cities of the duchy; one at the bridge of Porta Romana with statues of river gods; one at the « crocetta » of Porta Romana with paintings of ancient Roman heroes; one at the Contrada degli Aurefici with colossal statues representing victory on land and on sea; and one at the Piazza del Duomo with reliefs of sovereigns of the house of Habsburg and, on top, an equestrian statue of Charles, his horse trampling a Moor and a (Red) Indian, while a Turk is about to fall under its hooves. Giulio Romano is said by Albicante, below, to have been in charge of planning the *apparati*, but none of his sketches for them seem to survive. Albicante has, however, simple woodcuts of four arches, and there are very good verbal descriptions, along with the texts of inscriptions. Various entertainments, including jousts, followed during the week of Charles' stay.

Sources

1. ALBICANTE, GIOVANNI ALBERTO, *Trattato del'intrar in Milano di Carlo V.C. sempre Aug. con le proprie figure de li archi, e per ordine, li nobili vassalli e prencipi e signori cesarei, fabbricato e composto per l'Albicante* [...]. Milano, Andrea Calvi 1541, 4°, cc. 26. Biblioteca Nazionale, Florence: Landau Finaly 226.

An affected account in *ottava rima* with, however, a detailed list of the procession, quite detailed descriptions of the *apparali*, the texts of inscriptions, and rather simple woodcuts of four triumphal arches. The author states that Giulio Romano was in charge of planning the *apparati*. The main source.

2. BUGATI, *Historia universale*, pp. 896-900.

A good account by a witness, with much description of the *apparati*, though no recording of inscriptions. Some information about later entertainments.

3. BURIGOZZO, *Cronica milanese*, pp. 545-547.

Some first-hand description of the procession, nothing on the *apparati*. A crucial page was missing in the ms. from which this publication comes.

4. SANTA CRUZ, *Crónica de Emperador Carlos V*, vol. IV, pp. 112-114.

Much information about the entry procession, including costumes, but little concerning the *apparati*.

5. VANDENESSE, *Journal des voyages de Charles-Quint*, pp. 189-190.

By a member of the emperor's household, a short account with some information on the procession and general remarks about the *apparati*.

Studies

6. JACQUOT, *Panorama des fêtes et cérémonies du règne*, p. 442 and plate XI, fig. 2, at the end of the volume.

A short analysis of some of the *apparati* and reproduction of one of Albicante's woodcuts of an arch.

7. STRONG, *Splendour at Court*, p. 97 and fig. 77.

A short discussion of the *apparati* with reproduction of one of Albicante's woodcuts of an arch.

8. TRECCANI, *Storia di Milano*, vol. X, pp. 918-920.

Long quotations from Bugati, above, mainly concerning costumes.

IX

1548, December 20-1549, January 7. ENTRY AND SOJOURN OF PRINCE PHILLIP OF SPAIN, ON HIS WAY TO GERMANY AND THE LOW COUNTRIES.

A very elaborate and well-documented entry, with sumptuous entertainments on the following days. Entry by the Porta Ticinese and procession to the Duomo and Corte, or Palazzo Ducale. Principal *apparati*: a triumphal arch at the Porta, with eight statues of cities of the duchy and paintings of episodes in the life of the prince; an arch apparently at the entrance of the Piazza del Duomo with statues of Habsburg sovereigns and the prince: another at the door of the Duomo with David, Goliath, and other biblical characters; another at the entrance of the Corte with statues of the prince, his father Charles V, Mercury, and Minerva. Apparently no drawings of the *apparati* survive, but there are detailed descriptions, and many inscriptions are recorded. The identity of the artists seems to be unknown. About December 30: playing of a comedy entitled *Gl'inganni* by Niccolò Secchi, a Milanese city official, with an elaborate stage setting representing Venice. (See, however, Gillet, below). Topical *intermedii* with a personified Italy and a Mercury who gave an oration to the prince. January 6: the playing of a second comedy, apparently the *Alessandro* of Alessandro Piccolomini, with a stage setting representing Pisa. Some theatre historians have thought that Luca Contile's *Cesarea Gonzaga* was also played for the prince. The marriage of the daughter of Ferrante Gonzaga, imperial governor of Milan, took place during the visit, and there were also banquets and at least one tournament.

Sources

1. ALBICANTE, GIOVANNI ALBERTO, *Al gran Maximiliano d'Austria granduca, intrada di Milano di Don Filippo d'Austria re di Spagna, capriccio d'historia de l'Albicante*. In Venetia, a le Case di Marcolini, n.d., but doubtless 1548 or 1549, 4º, cc. 40. Biblioteca Nazionale Braidense, Milan: ZCC. 3.78, n. 1.

A long, affected account in *ottava rima* by the author of a description of the earlier entry of Charles V in 1541. Much attention to the procession with flattering mentions of many important personages. Very good description of the *apparati* with the text of inscriptions. A good account of later entertainments, including the playing of the two comedies, only the second of which, Piccolomini's, is identified. Includes the text (probably adapted) of verses recited to the prince by the children of Ferrante Gonzaga after the second performance. A major source.

2. ALVAREZ, *Relación del camino del Principe D. Felipe*, exact reference not known.

Not seen. Quoted by Gillet, below, in regard to the first comedy performance. Apparently a major source.

3. BUGATI, *Historia universale*, pp. 959-961.

A very good witness account. Much on the city's preparations for the entry. Some description of the *apparati*, without inscriptions. Some information about the later entertainments, including a very enthusiastic account of the playing of Secchi's comedy.

4. CALVETE, *El felicissimo viaje*, cc. 21r-33r.

A detailed and systematic account by the historian of the prince's journey. Good descriptions of the *apparati*, recording of many inscriptions, and much information on later entertainments. The author records the playing of the two comedies, with some description of their settings, but without noting titles or the names of the authors. A major source.

5. NOBILI, ALBERTO DE', *La triumphale entrata del serenissimo prence di Spagna nell'inclitta città di Melano il di. xix di decembre M.D.XLVIII*. N.p., n.d., but doubtless 1548 or 1549, 4º, cc. 6. Biblioteca Nazionale Braidense, Milano: ZCC. 3. 78, n. 2.

A witness account of the entry, apparently written the same day, with quite good descriptions of the *apparati*, including some measurements and the text of inscriptions, and a list of the procession. A major source.

6. SANTA CRUZ, *Crónica del Emperador Carlos V*, vol. V, pp. 241-248 and 253-256.

By the would-be Spanish historian of the emperor's reign, a very full account of the prince's visit, with good description of the entry *apparati* and the text of inscriptions in

Spanish translation. Considerable information as well about later entertainments, including the playing of the two comedies. Perhaps derived mainly from Calvete.

7. [SECCHI, NICCOLO], *Gl'inganni, comedia del Signor N.S., recitata in Milano l'anno 1547 [sic] dinanzi alla maestà del Re Filippo, nuovamente posta in luce.* Firenze, Giunti 1582 (but 1586 on last page), 16°, pp. 103. Biblioteca Nazionale, Firenze: Palatina 12.5.2.37.

The first edition of the comedy by Secchi most theatre historians have thought was presented before the prince. (See, however, Gillet, below). The prologue makes no reference to the circumstances of the production, and the topical *intermedii* are not included.

8. ULLOA, *Vita e fatti dell'invittissimo Imperatore Carlo V*, cc. 184r-186r.

A good summary of the occasion, with the recording of some inscriptions. The information may come mainly from Calvete, above, but it is also possible that the author was present (as he was at later stages of the prince's journey).

Studies

9. CREIZENACH, *Geschichte des Neueren Dramas*, Band II, Theil I, p. 331.

States that Secchi's *Gl'inganni* was not performed before Phillip.

10. *Enciclopedia della spettacolo*, under « Milano », vol. VII, col. 550.

A mention of the production of two comedies in the « sala del Senato del Palazzo Ducale ».

11. GILLET, JOSEPH E., *Was Secchi's « Gl'inganni » performed before Phillip of Spain?* « Modern Language Notes », vol. XXXV, 1920, pp. 393-401.

Basing himself on a witness account of the first performance by Vicente Alvarez (listed above as « not seen »), the author argues convincingly that the first comedy performed before the prince was not that of Secchi known today as *Gl'inganni* but another of the same author known now as *L'interesse*. He believes that Secchi had not assigned firm titles to the plays himself and that a posthumous editor gave that of *Gl'inganni*, associated with the performance in Milan, to the wrong play. *L'interesse*, which he thinks was the original *Gl'inganni*, was first published in Venice by Francesco Ziletti in 1581.

12. JACQUOT, *Panorama des fêtes et cérémonies du règne*, pp. 442-444.

A valuable analysis of the *apparati*.

13. MANGO, *La commedia in lingua*, pp. 126-127, 142-143, and 173-174.

Descriptions of the first editions of *Gl'inganni* (1562), *Alessandro* (1545), and the *Cesarea Gonzaga* (1550), with analyses of the plays, information on their first productions, and short bibliographies. The author does not think that the *Alessandro* was presented before the prince, as now seems demonstrated by Nicolini, below, while he believes that the *Cesarea Gonzaga* was.

14. NICOLINI, *Sul viaggio di Filippo d'Asburgo in Italia*, pp. 234 and 240-260.

A very good summary of events, based on all the important sources, including some ms. ones. Considerable attention to the *apparati* and a very valuable discussion of the productions of *Gl'inganni* and *Alessandro*. The author seems to establish definitely the fact of the second production.

15. SANESI, *La commedia*, vol. I, pp. 314-315, 328-330, and 393-395.

Analyses of Secchi's *Gl'inganni* (which the author thinks was not put on for the occasion), of Contile's *Cesarea Gonzaga* (which he thinks was done), and of Piccolomini's *Alessandro* (which he does not mention as having been done).

16. SAXL, F., *Costumes and Festivals of Milanese Society under Spanish Rule*. From the « Proceedings of the British Academy », vol. XXIII. London, Humphrey Milford Amen House 1936, pp. 5-21, 41-48, and plates 3, 4, 8, 9, 11, 12, 16, 17, 20, 21, and 27.

The author discusses a sixteenth-century Milanese tailor's book of costume illustrations which includes, he believes, some of those worn on the occasion of Prince Phillip's visit. He also gives some information about the entry and visit, with quotations from Albicante's account, and in an appendix gives abstracts of a number of relative documents he has seen in the archives of Milan, Mantua, Modena, Parma, and Siena.

17. TRECCANI, *Storia di Milano*, vol. IX, pp. 131-132, and vol. X, pp. 920-921.

Information on the political circumstances of the prince's visit and valuable references to three ms. sources, one of which, a report of the Ferrara ambassador Trotta, is quoted at length.

18. VIANELLO, C., *Feste, tornei, congiure nel Cinquecento milanese*, « Archivio Storico Lombardo », nuova serie, anno I, 1936, pp. 381-389.

A summary of the celebrations, with most attention to the procession and the comedy productions and little to the *apparati*. Based on the published accounts of Albicante and Nobili, above, and on a ms. account in the Biblioteca Ambrosiana, Milan.

NAPLES

I

1494, May 8. CORONATION OF KING ALFONSO II.

The coronation celebrations, which had been preceded the day
before by the marriage of the king's daughter Sancha to Goffre
Borgia, son of Pope Alexander VI, included a ride from the Castello
to the Duomo, elaborate coronation rites, and a solemn ride afterward
around the five *seggi* of the city. Principal *apparati*: an elaborate
« teatro » inside the Duomo, and, at the Mint, opposite Sant'Agostino
church, a representation of Orpheus with his lyre charming animals
and inanimate objects. The head of the Mint had also built a horn
of plenty that poured out coins on the king's passage.

Sources

1. GIACOMO, *Cronaca di Napoli*, p. 181.
A sparse account of the coronation.

2. PASSERO, *Giornale*, pp. 60-61.
A good witness' account of the ceremonies and the procession to the *seggi*.

3. PELLICCIA, *Raccolta di varie croniche*, tomo I, pp. 38, 154, 182, 197, 292.
Several short accounts of the ceremonies.

Studies

4. MAGISTRETTI, PIETRO, *Lutto e feste alla corte di Napoli, relazione diplo-
matica dell'ambasciatore milanese al duca di Bari*. « Archivio Storico Lombardo »,
anno VI, 1879, pp. 685-720.

Prints letters from the Archivio di Stato in Milan that contain, among other things,
a very detailed account of the investiture ceremonies and much description of costumes.

5.   PERCOPO, E., *Notizie della coronazione di Alfonso II d'Aragona*, « Archivio Storico per le Province Napoletane », Anno XIV, 1889, pp. 140-143.

A summary of the festivities taken mainly from Summonte, but with some references to other sources.

6.   PONTIERI, *Storia di Napoli*, vol. IV, tomo I, p. 264.

A short account of the coronation with bibliographical references.

7.   SUMMONTE, *Dell'historia della città e regno di Napoli*, tomo III, pp. 482-495.

An excellent detailed account based on ms. sources. Includes the text of some of the ceremonial in the Duomo. Some interesting information on *apparati*.

II

1495, February 22 and May 12. ENTRIES OF KING CHARLES VIII OF FRANCE AS CONQUEROR AND KING OF THE REALM.

February 22: a simple entry because the king had not wished to wait until the 25th so that the Neapolitans could prepare *apparati*, which were to include a triumphal chariot. The king entered from the Poggio Reale with a small company and rode around the city, perhaps stopping at the Duomo, before settling at the Palazzo Capuano. The Castel Nuovo was still in the hands of Aragonese forces. On May 12 he made a second, solemn entry before his departure from the city. Entry from the Poggio Reale under a *baldacchino*, wearing a crown and carrying the orb and sceptre. Elaborate procession, with French and Neapolitan dignitaries, going around to the five *seggi*, where the king was awaited by local officials, and then to the Duomo. Inside, there were elaborate ceremonies, including an oath by the king to uphold the rights of the citizens, and perhaps an oration by the humanist Giovanni Pontano speaking for the Neapolitans. There was, however, almost certainly no actual coronation, the king having been unable to obtain investiture from the pope. Little is known of the *apparati* in the streets.

Sources

1. ANONYMOUS EDITOR, *Nuovi documenti francesi sulla impresa di Carlo VIII.* « Archivio Storico per le Province Napoletane », nuova serie, anno XXIV, 1938, pp. 183-257.

Publishes a large number of letters written home by Frenchmen in Naples around the time of the second entry but captured by the Milanese and now in the Archivio di Stato of Milan. A large proportion of them contain accounts of the second entry with a good deal of precise information. The most interesting of these are found on pp. 205-207, 213-214, 224-227, 230-231, 249-250, and 253-254. A major source.

2. ANONYMOUS, *Racconti di storia napoletana.* « Archivio Storico per le Province Napoletane », vol. XXXIII, 1908, pp. 514-518.

Some information on both entries, with an erroneous statement that Charles was crowned by a papal legate.

3. ANONYMOUS, *Sensuyt lentree et couronnement du roy nostre sire en sa ville de Napples faicte le xxii. jour de fevrier mil. cccc iiii xx et xiiii.* N.p., n.d., but doubtless 1495, 4°, cc. 3. Bibliothèque Nationale, Paris: Rés. Lb²⁸. 1. Reprinted in LA PILORGERIE, *Campagnes et bulletins*, pp. 200-205.

A highly interesting but quite unreliable source. Apparently a newsheet on the first entry sent back to France. The author mentions a machine at the city gate by which two children dressed as angels descended from the sky and presented a crown to the king. It recounts ceremonies in the Duomo not mentioned by other sources, and an actual coronation in the «palace of King Alfonso» that almost certainly did not take place. The sheet was apparently prepared for the purpose of propaganda.

4. CHARLES VIII, king of France, a letter from Naples dated February 12 addressed to his ambassadors in Rome, printed in GODEFROY, *Histoire de Charles VIII*, p. 716.

The king informs the ambassadors of his first entry and of having received the « obéissance, serment et fidélité » of the Neapolitans.

5. GIACOMO, *Cronaca di Napoli*, pp. 187-190.

A little information on the first entry and a bit more on the procession for the second.

6. GUICCIARDINI, *Storia d'Italia*, vol. I, p. 147.

States that on the occasion of the second entry Giovanni Pontano spoke in the Duomo as the representative of the Neapolitans.

7

7.   LA VIGNE, *Vergier d'honneur*, in the ca. 1500 edition, cc. k 1r and l 3v-l 5r; in Cimber's edition, pp. 336 and 360-362; *Histoire du voyage de Naples*, pp. 132 and 146-148, printed also in GODEFROY, *Le Cérémonial françois*, tome I, 682-684; *La Très Curieuse et Chevaleresque Hystoire*, pp. 68 and 93-95.

Quite short reports of the first entry and a good deal more about the second, in which the king is said to have entered « en habit impérial et appelé Auguste ». The ca. 1500 edition of the *Vergier* has several woodcuts alluding to triumphal entries but none seem to refer specifically to Naples.

8.   PASSERO, *Giornale*, pp. 68-72.

Little on the first entry but more on the procession around the *seggi* for the second.

9.   PELLICCIA, *Raccolta di varie croniche*, tomo I, p. 221.

A short witness account of the second entry.

10.   SANUDO, *La spedizione di Carlo VIII in Italia*, pp. 233-236.

A short account of the first entry, and of the Neapolitans' frustrated preparations. Nothing on the second.

Studies

11.   CHERRIER, *Histoire de Charles VIII*, tome II, pp. 132-133 and 176-179.

Good summaries of the two entries.

12.   DELABORDE, *L'Expédition de Charles VIII en Italie*, pp. 555-556 and 602-603.

Good systematic account of both entries based on nearly all the important sources.

13.   PONTIERI, *Storia di Napoli*, vol. V, tomo I, pp. 268-272.

An account of Charles' stay, with some specific information on the May 12 entry.

14.   PERCOPO, ERASMO, *Per l'entrata solenne di Carlo VIII in Napoli*, in *Studi di storia napoletana in onore di Michelangelo Schipa*. Napoli, I.T.E.A. Editrice 1926, pp. 347-352.

Publishes a letter of the very anti-French Milanese ambassador, Girolamo Tuttavilla, to Ascanio Sforza, dated May 13, describing the entry. The editor supplies some additional information of his own.

15.   LA PILORGERIE, *Campagne et bulletins*, pp. 187-205 and 272-274.

Summaries of the two entries with publication of several letters written to France by the king and other Frenchmen, and of the unreliable news bulletin *Sensuyt lentree et couronnement* listed above.

16. SUMMONTE, *Dell'historia della città et regno di Napoli*, tomo III, pp. 512-514 and 517.

A summary of the first entry and a brief reference to the second.

III

1506, November 1. ENTRY OF KING FERDINAND OF SPAIN AND HIS QUEEN GERMAINE DE FOIX.

An elaborate entry with important *apparati*. The king landed at the port, where a long pier, decorated with « storie antiche », had been built into the sea. On the dock, a « teatro », or « tabernacolo », or « arco », with thrones and, on top, five nymphs holding banners. Dispute over precedence for carrying the *baldacchino*. Procession around the *seggi*, each of which had decorations and representatives of the nobility of the area, to the Duomo and to the Castello. There were at least two triumphal arches, not properly seen because noblemen jealous of those who had commissioned them managed to have the route of the procession changed. One arch had figures of Mars, Janus, and Jacob, as well as real men tossing coins. By the church of Sant'Agostino, a nobleman and his wife waited to greet the sovereigns, while their children, dressed as angels, sang words of welcome. *Apparato* also at the door of the Castello. Little is known of the iconography of the various decorations, and inscriptions are not preserved.

Sources

1. FUSCOLILLO, GASPARE, *Le cronache de li antiqui ri del regno di Napoli di D. Gaspare Fuscolillo*, a cura di Bartolomeo Capasso. « Archivio Storico per le Province Napoletane », anno I, 1876, pp. 76-77.

A witness account with some information on the *apparati*.

2. GIACOMO, *Cronaca di Napoli*, pp. 289-293.

An interesting witness account with some specific information on the *apparati* and frank report of several contretemps that occurred during the ceremonies.

3. MEDINA, GIOVANNI, letter to the Cardinal d'Este dated November 8, published by RICCARDO FILANGIERI, *Arrivo di Ferdinando il Cattolico a Napoli (Relazione dell'oratore Giovanni Medina al Cardinal d'Este)*, in *Fernando el Católico y Italia*. Zaragoza, Institución El Católico 1954 (V Congreso de Historia de la Corona de Aragón, Zaragoza 4-11 de octubre 1952), pp. 311-314.

A very interesting account with numerous details about the ceremonies and *apparati*.

4. PASSERO, *Giornale*, pp. 146-147.

A short witness account, with much information on costumes, something about the « tabernacolo » at the port and about the procession.

5. PELLICCIA, *Raccolta di varie croniche*, tomo I, pp. 41, 197-198, 246, and 282.

Short recordings of the entry.

6. SANTA CRUZ, ALONSO DE, *Crónica de los reyes católicos (hasta ahora inédita)*, edición y estudio preliminar por Juan De Mata Carriazo. Sevilla, Escuela de Estudios Hispano-Americanos 1951, tomo II, pp. 72-74.

Quite a good account of the entry, with considerable information on the *apparati*, by a contemporary Spanish historian who clearly had access to first-hand descriptions.

7. SANUDO, *Diarii*, vol. VI, cols. 481-483.

A valuable summary of the entry from letters sent to Venice.

Studies

8. PONTIERI, *Storia di Napoli*, vol. IV, tomo I, p. 9.

A very short account of the entry with, however, a number of bibliographical references in the notes.

9. SUMMONTE, *Dell'historia della città e regno di Napoli*, tomo IV, pp. 4-5.

A sparse account of the occasion.

IV

1535, November 25-1536, March 27. ENTRY AND SOJOURN OF EM-
PEROR CHARLES V DURING HIS TRIUMPHAL PROGRESS UP THROUGH
ITALY AFTER THE VICTORY OF TUNIS.

A well-documented entry whose *apparati* have a particularly
dense (not always clearly coherent) iconographical content and
numerous interesting inscriptions. The emperor was met by city officials and church dignitaries at the Porta Capuana. Procession to the
Seggio di Capuana and the Duomo, which he entered for prayer and
to swear to protect the privileges of the citizens. Thence to the Piazza
di San Lorenzo, Piazza di Sant'Agostino and the Castel Nuovo,
where he was to stay. Principal *apparati*: (1) decorations of Porta
Capuana, including statues of San Gennaro and Sant'Agnello, patrons of the city, and a welcoming inscription; (2) a triumphal arch,
apparently just within the gate, with a dense iconography of statues (including Scipio Africanus Major, Julius Caesar, Alexander
the Great, Hannibal, and four Habsburg emperors) and many paintings showing, among other things, scenes of victories in Africa and
Central Europe, mythological creatures, and emblems of abstract
qualities (e.g. Charles receiving the king of France as an emblem of
Humanitas); (3) colossal statues erected along the route by the various
seggi (e.g. Mars and Jove for the Seggio di Capuana); (4) in the
Strada della Sellaria a machine showing Giants mounting up to
Heaven to challenge Jove being struck by a thunderbolt launched
by an imperial eagle; (5) a long inscription over the door of the Castel Nuovo. No works of art or preparatory drawings seem to survive, and the names of the participating artists are apparently not
known, but the written descriptions are full, and many inscriptions
are recorded. During the emperor's stay there were many entertainments, including jousts, bullfights and races and, apparently, the
performance of a comedy, which may have been the *farsa cavaiola*
entitled *Ricevuta dell'imperatore alla Cava* (see the *Enciclopedia dello
spettacolo* and Sanesi below).

Sources

1. ANONYMOUS, *Racconti di storia napoletana*. « Archivio Storico per le Province Napoletane », vol. XXXIV, 1909, pp. 115-117.

Contains detailed information about the immediate preliminaries to Charles' entry, but the editor does not include the author's description of the entry itself, which he says is similar to those of Castaldo and Summonte. Reference to the ms. of the description.

2. ANONYMOUS, *Relation de l'entrée de Charles-Quint dans la ville de Naples: 25 novembre, 1535*. In GACHARD, *Collection des voyages des souverains des Pays-Bas*, tome II, pp. 573-581.

By a French-speaking soldier in the service of the emperor, a naïve but rather detailed description of the *apparati*, with the inscriptions given in French translation.

3. ANONYMOUS, *Le suntuose feste, giostre, giochi di canne, caccie di tori, e carrere di corsieri fatte in la inclita città di Napoli alla presentia della Cesarea Maestà col lo apparato della piazza e ordine della festa. Et delle diverse carrete livree e fogie fatte agarra dalle signore e gentildonne del regno*. N.p., n.d., but probably Naples 1536, 4°, cc. 6. Biblioteca Riccardiana, Florence: Moreniana B 5 64.

An account of jousts, bullfights and other entertainments held in the presence of the emperor in the Piazza San Giovanni di Carbonara in early January. Interesting descriptions of chariots that bought the emperor's daughter Margherita d'Austria and other ladies to the spectacle.

4. CASTALDO, ANTONINO, *Dell'historia di notar Antonino Castaldo libri quattro*. In GRAVIER, *Raccolta di tutti i più rinomati scrittori*, tomo VI, pp. 48-59.

A good, detailed witness description of the *apparati*, with many inscriptions, and an interesting report of popular speculation about the meaning of some of the iconography. A good account as well of the entertainments that took place during the emperor's stay. A major source.

5. DANZA, PAULO, *Il triomphale apparato per la entrata de la Cesarea Maesta in Napoli, con tutte le particolarita, archi triomphali, statue antiche, cosa bellissima*. N.p., n.d., but doubtless 1535, 4°, cc. 4. British Museum, London: 1057. h. 25 (2).

A systematic account with detailed, if telegraphic, description of the *apparati* and the texts of inscriptions. Some information also on the entry procession, including costumes. A major source.

6. MONTOICHE, *Voyage et expédition de Charles-Quint au pays de Tunis*, pp. 384-386.

Probably by a soldier in the service of the emperor, a short account with general references to the *apparati*.

7. PELLICCIA, *Raccolta di varie croniche*, tomo I, pp. 43-44.

In the chronicles of Tommaso de Catania, a page on the entry, with reference to the most important *apparati*. Notes that the arch at Porta di Santa Caterina cost the Seggio di Capuana 3,000 ducati.

8. ROSSO, GREGORIO, *Istoria delle cose di Napoli sotto l'imperio di Carlo V*. In GRAVIER, *Raccolta di tutti i più rinomati scrittori*, tomo VIII, pp. 58-70.

An informative account by a Neapolitan city official who was involved in the preparations and ceremonies of the entry. No systematic description of the *apparati* because the author is writing several years later, but many recalled details about the procession and ceremonies, and some information on the later entertainments during Charles' stay.

9. [SALA, ANDREA], *Triomphi ordinati in la citta di Napoli in la entrata di la Cesarea Maesta*. In SALA's *La triomphale entrata di Carlo. V. imperadore augusto en la inclita citta di Napoli e di Missina*, cc. A1r-C4v.

A very careful account, with good descriptions of the *apparati* and recording of many inscriptions, by the author of the descriptions of the entries into Messina, Siena, and Florence. The main source.

10. SANTA CRUZ, *Crónica del Emperador Carlos V*, vol. III, pp. 304-316.

A very detailed account of the entry, with much description of the *apparati* and much explanation of their historical and mythological allusions. The author (who hoped to become the emperor's official historiographer) was probably not present but must have used detailed contemporary sources.

11. VANDENESSE, *Journal des voyages de Charles-Quint*, pp. 115-116.

A sparse report by a member of the emperor's household.

12. VASARI, in the life of Antonio da San Gallo, *Opere*, vol. V, p. 464.

A disappointing passing reference to the entry, with no information on the *apparati* and no mention of the artists who worked on them.

Studies

13. *Enciclopedia dello spettacolo*, under « Napoli », vol. VII, p. 1008.

States that a comedy was presented before the emperor on February 2 and suggests that it may have been the farce *Ricevuta dell'imperatore alla Cava*.

14. JACQUOT, *Panorama des fêtes et cérémonies du règne*, pp. 430-431.

A short analysis of the *apparati*.

15. PONTIERI, *Storia di Napoli*, vol. V, tomo I, pp. 53-57.

An account of Charles' stay with a small amount of information on the entry.

16. SANESI, *La commedia*, vol. I, pp. 442-444.

An analysis of *La ricevuta dell'imperatore alla Cava*, which is the only surviving example of the popular genre called the *farsa cavaiola*. The author does not conjecture that it was presented before Charles V, but its subject, the reception of the emperor in the stock « hick town » of Cava, near Salerno, was highly topical and would have been a most appropriate entertainment.

17. STRONG, *Splendour at Court*, p. 94.

A quite short examination of the entry.

18. SUMMONTE, *Dell'historia della città e regno di Napoli*, tomo II, pp. 91-123.

A very full account based on documents in the Neapolitan archives and perhaps also on Sala, above. Very detailed descriptions of the *apparati*, mention of all the inscriptions with full Italian translations but abbreviation of some of the original Latin texts.

PAVIA

I

1494, October 14. Entry of King Charles VIII of France, on His Way to Conquer the Kingdom of Naples.

An elaborate but poorly documented entry. There were apparently some triumphal arches, and some *mystères*, with biblical characters, were played in the streets on the king's passage. Verses may also have been recited to explain the *apparati*. Descriptions of the decorations and *mystères* are poor, and no verses or inscriptions seem to have been recorded. While in Pavia the king visited the dying Duke Giangaleazzo Sforza of Milan.

Sources

1. Desrey, *Relation du voyage de Naples*, in the Godefroy ed., p. 201; in the Cimber ed., p. 216.

Some information on the procession by a witness.

2. Grumello, Antonio, *Cronaca di Antonio Grumello pavese* [...], pubblicata per la prima volta dal Professore Giuseppe Müller. Milano, Francesco Colombo 1856 («Raccolta di cronisti e documenti storici lombardi inediti», 1), pp. 5-6.

An enthusiastic, but undetailed witness account of the king's entry and information about other events during his stay.

3. La Vigne, *Vergier d'honneur*, ca. 1500 ed., cc. f1v-f2r, under the erroneous heading «Commant le roy fut receu a Pyse»; *Histoire du voyage de Naples*,

p. 115; *La Très Curieuse et Chevaleresque Hystoire de la conqueste de Naples*, pp. 32-34.

The main source, with some unfortunately vague information about the procession, the *apparati* and the *mystères*.

Studies

4.   CHERRIER, *Histoire de Charles VIII*, tome I, p. 461.

A summary of the entry with brief mention of the *apparati*.

5.   DELABORDE, *L'Expédition de Charles VIII en Italie*, p. 418.

A brief recording of the king's passage.

II

1507, May 18. ENTRY OF KING LOUIS XII OF FRANCE, AFTER HIS RE-CONQUEST OF GENOA.

A rather elaborate entry by Ponte del Ticino, with procession to the Duomo and Castello. Principal *apparati*: decorations of the bridge, including a « tabernacle de verdure », and inscriptions. There were at least one other « tabernacle » and a number of inscriptions along the streets. Giorgio di Candia, a student living in the city, is said to have written Latin verses that were posted along the route. Fairly good descriptions of the *apparati* and procession and the texts of inscriptions survive.

Sources

1.   AUTON, *Chroniques*, Tome IV, pp. 60-65.

A rather full account by the king's historian, who was present. There is some description of the simple *apparati*, and a number of inscriptions and verses posted along the way are recorded. The main source.

2.   SANUDO, *Diarii*, vol. VII, cols. 80 and 83.

Brief accounts of the king's entry, with general allusions to the *apparati*.

III

1548, December 17. ENTRY OF PRINCE PHILLIP OF SPAIN, ON HIS WAY TO GERMANY AND THE LOW COUNTRIES.

Entry by the Ponte del Ticino and procession to the Castello. Principal *apparati*: three triumphal arches, of which the first was at the entry to the bridge, with welcoming inscriptions. On the next day the humanist Andrea Alciati, a famous authority on emblems, gave a Latin oration. On leaving the city, the prince visited the battlefield where Francis I had been taken prisoner in 1525. The entry inscriptions are preserved.

Sources

1. ALVAREZ, *Relación del camino del Principe D. Felipe*, exact reference unknown.

Not seen. Since the author was a member of the prince's party, this may be an important source.

2. CALVETE, *El felicissimo viaje*, cc. 19v-20v.

By the Spanish historian of the prince's journey, a short account that is the source of nearly all our information.

3. SANTA CRUZ, *Crónica del Emperador Carlos V*, vol. V, p. 241.

A bare recording of the prince's visit.

Study

4. NICOLINI, *Sul viaggio di Filippo d'Asburgo in Italia*, pp. 233-234.

A short account of the prince's visit.

PISA

I

1494, November 8-10, and 1495, June 20-23. ENTRIES AND SOJOURNS OF KING CHARLES VIII OF FRANCE, ON HIS WAY TO CONQUER THE KINGDOM OF NAPLES AND DURING HIS RETURN JOURNEY TOWARD FRANCE.

The Pisans seized occasions of the king's visits to try to win their freedom from Florence, and that makes their receptions of him – even the second one, during the return journey, which was anticlimactic in other cities – particularly poignant. In the entry of November 8, 1494, there was a grand procession and the king was greeted as a liberator. The streets were decorated at least with tapestries and coats of arms, and there may have been *mystères* played on his passage. The next day a delegation of citizens went to ask the king for the city's freedom, under his protection. He gave an ambiguous answer that was taken as affirmative, and the Pisans then tore down a Marzocco lion, symbol of Florentine domination, on a bridge over the Arno. That night they celebrated in front of the king's residence. For the second entry, June 20, 1495, the Pisans, who hoped to keep their liberty despite now evident hesitation on the part of the king, had prepared a triumphal arch and an equestrian statue of the monarch with his horse trampling a lion and a serpent, which represented Florence and Duke Ludovico il Moro of Milan. At a ball on the next day, well-born ladies of the city fell at the king's feet to beg for the freedom of their city. The king, who, like the French chroniclers of the occasion, had been moved by the Pisan entreaties, now made no promises. Nevertheless, by dint of courage and hard fighting, the city was able to preserve its independence for several years thereafter. The artists for these entries are not known, no drawings seem to survive, and the accounts are disappointingly short.

Sources

1. COMINES, *Mémoires*, tome III, pp. 56-60.

Interesting details about the 1494 reception of the king, which Comines had learned about from dispatches sent to Venice.

2. DESREY, *Relation du voyage du Roy Charles VIII*, in the Godefroy ed., pp. 203-204; in the Cimber ed., p. 220.

A brief account of the 1494 entry with emphasis on the Pisans' pleas for liberty.

3. GUICCIARDINI, *Storia d'Italia*, vol. I, pp. 150-151.

An account of the Pisans' reception of Charles and of their entreaties to him, from the Florentine point of view.

4. LA VIGNE, *Vergier d'honneur*, in the ca. 1500 ed., for 1494, cc. f6r-g3v (erroneously headed « Sensuyt commant le Roy entra a Pavye »), and for 1495, cc. m1r-m1v, reprinted in the Cimber ed., tome I, pp. 372-374; *Histoire du voyage de Naples*, p. 117 (1494) and pp. 153-154 (1495); *La Très Curieuse et Chevaleresque Hystoire de la conqueste de Naples*, pp. 34-43 (1494) and ca. p. 101 (1495).

The best witness accounts with most of our information on the processions and *apparati*. The ca. 1500 edition of the *Vergier d'honneur* has woodcuts that may allude to the 1494 entry.

5. PORTOVENERI, GIOVANNI, *Memoriale di Giovanni Portoveneri dall'anno 1494 sino al 1502*. « Archivio Storico Italiano », tomo VI, parte 2ª, 1845, pp. 286-288 (1494) and 313-314 (1495).

A good deal of information about events during the king's two visits, with an allusion to the *apparati* for the second.

6. SANUDO, *La spedizione di Carlo V in Italia*, pp. 111-114 (1494) and 421-422 (1495).

A good deal of information about the king's doings, including his negotiations with the Pisans during the first visit.

Studies

7. CHERRIER, *Histoire de Charles VIII*, tome II, pp. 18-23 (1494) and 201-202 (1495).

Good accounts of the king's two visits with some attention to the ceremonies and *apparati*.

8. DELABORDE, *L'Expédition de Charles VIII en Italie*, pp. 447 (1494) and 620 (1495).

Short accounts of the king's two visits with no attention to ceremonies or the *apparati*.

9. LA PILORGERIE, *Campagnes et bulletins*, pp. 94-97 (1494) and 298-304 (1495).

The author's own narration of events during the first visit and publication of a letter written by the king from Pisa during the second visit.

10. LUPO-GENTILE, M., *Pisa, Firenze e Carlo VIII*. Pisa, Nistri-Lischi 1934, pp. 11-16 (1494) and 52-56 (1495).

Good summaries of events during the king's two visits, with emphasis on political discussions. Based on all the important sources.

ROME

I

1494, December 31-1495, January 28. ENTRY AND SOJOURN OF KING CHARLES VIII OF FRANCE, ON HIS WAY TO CONQUER THE KINGDOM OF NAPLES.

A momentous and highly dramatic royal visit but a relatively uninteresting one from the point of view of artistic and other cultural manifestations. The king entered the city by the Porta del Popolo, at the head of his army, in the evening of December 31, before he was expected and before the Romans had had time to make appropriate arrangements. He proceeded to the Palazzo San Marco, which had been prepared for his residence. Pope Alexander VI was at first fearful of meeting the king, but the two did greet each other at the Vatican Palace on January 16, and there were several other meetings thereafter. The pope and the king rode through the city together on January 25, and there were also several religious ceremonies in churches.

Sources

1. ANONYMOUS AND OF VARIOUS AUTHORSHIP, *Recueil de pièces du temps de Charles VIII*. N.p., n.d., but probably Paris 1495. Bibliothèque Nationale, Paris: Rés. Lb28. 1. Several news sheets published to give the French people news of the king's progress in Italy. Those relevant to Rome reprinted in LA PILORGERIE, *Campagnes et bulletins*, pp. 144-153.

Includes a brief account of the entry entitled *Lentree du roy nostre sire a Rome*, letters written by Charles himself to his brother Monseigneur de Bourbon, an account of the meeting of the king and the pope, articles of agreement between the two, and the account of a pontifical mass attended by the king. The information is in general not very detailed.

2.   BURCHARD, *Liber notarum*, vol. I, pp. 558-574. Printed also in CIMBER, *Archives curieuses de l'histoire de France*, tome I, pp. 267-301, with facing French translation.

The author, papal master of ceremonies, had gone hastily out to meet Charles to discuss arrangements and found himself accompanying the king – and answering rapid-fire questions – during the entry. He gives a rather detailed account of events during the royal visit, from the Roman point of view and with his usual obsession for questions of ceremony and precedence. A major source.

3.   LA VIGNE, *Vergier d'honneur*, ca. 1500 ed., cc. h5v-i3r; *Histoire du voyage de Naples*, pp. 122-127; *La Très Curieuse et Chevaleresque Hystoire*, pp. 52-59.

Descriptions of the entry procession and a good deal of information on other events during the king's visit. The *Vergier d'honneur* has several woodcuts, of which one shows two kneeling prelates greeting the king. A major source.

4.   SANUDO, *La spedizione di Carlo VIII in Italia*, pp. 163-171.

Considerable information on the entry procession and on events during the king's stay, doubtless derived mainly from dispatches sent to Venice.

5.   TEDALLINI, *Diario romano*, p. 489.

A short account of events during the king's stay.

Studies

6.   CHERRIER, *Histoire de Charles VIII*, tome I, pp. 76-79.

A good summary of the entry, with quotations from Burchard.

7.   DELABORDE, *L'Expédition de Charles VIII en Italie*, pp. 507-526.

Little on the entry, but a very good modern account of events during the king's stay.

8.   LA PILORGERIE, *Campagnes et bulletins*, pp. 112-168.

A good summary of events, with publication of the *Recueil* of news bulletins cited above and of some additional letters written home by Frenchmen in Rome.

9.   PASTOR, *Storia dei papi*, vol. III, pp. 395-404.

A good account of the entry procession and of the later meetings of the king and the pope. Numerous bibliographical references.

II

1501, December 23-1503, January 6. FESTIVITIES FOR THE MARRIAGE OF LUCREZIA BORGIA, DAUGHTER OF POPE ALEXANDER VI, AND ALFONSO D'ESTE, SON OF DUKE ERCOLE I OF FERRARA.

Extremely elaborate civic and courtly entertainments. December 23: entry by the Porta del Popolo of Cardinal Ippolito d'Este, at the head of a delegation from Ferrara coming to fetch the bride. Elaborate ceremonies at the gate and procession to the Vatican without, apparently, any important *apparati* in the streets. By command of the pope, the Roman carnival began that year in December. Also on the 23rd: a ball in Lucrezia's palace. December 30: marriage ceremony in the Vatican; games, with a naumachia, in the Piazza San Pietro; and, that evening in the Vatican, a banquet, a ball, and the presentation of two « comedies », or dramatic skits, in Latin. December 31: allegorical skits in the houses of the Cardinal San Severino and Cesare Borgia, that in the latter being an eclogue exalting the Borgia and Este families. January 1: celebration of the Festa dell'Agone, with thirteen triumphal chariots representing, among other things, the triumphs of Julius Caesar, Paulus Aemilius, and Scipio Africanus Major. The chariots came to Piazza San Pietro, where explanatory verses were recited. In the evening, performance of comedies and *moresche* in the Vatican. January 2: a bull fight in Piazza San Pietro with Cesare Borgia among the participants and, in the evening, performance in the Vatican of Plautus' *Menaechmi* and of an allegorical skit featuring Rome and Ferrara. January 6: departure of Lucrezia for Ferrara with a large suite. The texts of the dramatic skits and the verses recited for the parade of chariots in Piazza San Pietro have apparently not survived. There are, however, rather good descriptions of the dramatic performances.

Sources

1. BURCHARD, *Liber notarum*, vol. II, pp. 307-316.

Much information on arrangements for the entry of Cardinal Ippolito, less on the later entertainments.

8

2. SANUDO, *Diarii*, vol. IV, cols. 195-199.

A letter describing the entry of Cardinal Ippolito and a detailed list of the suite of persons who accompanied Lucrezia to Ferrara.

3. TEDALLINI, *Diario romano*, pp. 296-297.

Some information on the arrival of the delegation from Ferrara and on Lucrezia's departure from Rome.

4. ZAMBOTTI, *Diario ferrarese*, pp. 310-311.

An account of the entry of the cardinal and his party into Rome.

Studies

5. CLEMENTI, *Carnevale romano*, pp. 106-112.

A very good account of the celebrations with many quotations from letters sent to Duke Ercole and to the Marchioness of Mantua Isabella d'Este.

6. D'ANCONA, *Origini del teatro italiano*, vol. II, pp. 73-75.

A brief general account, with reproduction of a letter to Duke Ercole describing the dramatic entertainments of January 2.

7. GREGOROVIUS, *Lucrezia Borgia*, pp. 209-224.

An excellent account of the festivities and ceremonies, based mainly on ms. letters from Este envoys addressed to the duke at home and to the Marchioness of Mantua Isabella d'Este. Some of the letters are quoted at length.

8. PASTOR, *Storia dei papi*, vol. III, p. 551.

A short account with bibliographical references.

III

1507, March 27-28 (Palm Sunday). TRIUMPHAL ENTRY OF POPE JULIUS II, AFTER A VICTORIOUS MILITARY CAMPAIGN IN WHICH HE HAD REGAINED BOLOGNA FOR THE PAPAL STATES.

A celebration remarkable for the High Renaissance promiscuity of Christian and classical pagan themes. On March 27 the pope was received at the Ponte Milvio by the senator and other city officials.

He spent the night at Santa Maria del Popolo, and on the next day, Sunday, March 28, he proceeded solemnly in three hours time from the Porta del Popolo to Saint Peter's through streets whose decorations evoked both a classical triumph and the entry of Christ into Jerusalem on Palm Sunday. There were triumphal arches, altars in front of churches, and a triumphal chariot holding both a globe and ten men waving olive branches. Apparently no drawings of the *apparati* remain, but numerous Latin inscriptions are recorded.

Sources

1. GRASSI, *Le due spedizioni militari di Giulio II*, pp. 168-176.

By the papal master of ceremonies, a very good account of preparations for the entry, including the author's ignored objections to the mixing of pagan and Christian themes, and good descriptions of several *apparati*.

2. SANUDO, *Diarii*, vol. VII, cols. 43 and 63-65.

A good report of the entry and a unique list of the inscriptions on various *apparati*.

3. TEDALLINI, *Diario romano*, p. 313.

A short report of the entry with mentions of the main *apparati*.

Studies

4. FIORANI, *Riti ceremonie feste*, pp. 141-142.

A good short account.

5. PASTOR, *Storia dei papi*, vol. III, pp. 721-722 and 1109-1110.

A very good summary of the entry, with reproduction of letters describing it sent to the duke of Ferrara and the marquess of Mantua.

6. RODOCANACHI, *Le Pontificat de Jules II*, pp. 79-80.

A good short account.

IV

1513, February 3. PARADE, DURING CARNIVAL, HONORING THE AC-COMPLISHMENTS OF POPE JULIUS II.

The parade, which came to Saint Peter's Square while the pope lay on his death bed in the Vatican, included sixteen triumphal chariots representing, among other things, cities captured by the pope (e.g. Bologna, Reggio Emilia, and Parma), an « Italia Liberata », the Lateran Council, and the Holy League.

Sources

1. ANONYMOUS, a letter to Battista Stabellini as transcribed and sent on by him to Isabella d'Este, reproduced in Alessandro Luzio, *Federico Gonzaga ostaggio alla corte di Giulio II.* « Archivio della R. Società Romana di Storia Patria », vol. IX, 1886, pp. 577-582.

Contains the most precise descriptions of some of the chariots.

2. PENNI, GIAN GIACOMO, *Magnifica et sumptuosa festa facta dalli S. R. per il carnovale M.D.XIII.* Originally probably published separately in an edition now lost; reproduced from a ms. by A. ADEMOLLO, *Alessandro VI, Giulio II e Leone X nel carnevale di Roma, documenti inediti (1499-1520)*. Firenze, C. Ademollo 1886, pp. 35-70.

A long poem in *ottava rima* with pedantic, circumlocutory language. Describes various carnival activities including, in considerable, though often unsystematic detail, the procession and the chariots.

Studies

3. CLEMENTI, *Carnevale romano*, pp. 125-138.

A very good summary based on Penni, above, and on some ms. letters, including that of Stabellini.

4. PASCHINI, *Roma nel Rinascimento*, pp. 402-403.

A short but precise account with mention of all the chariots.

5. RODOCANACHI, *Le Pontificat de Jules II*, pp. 177-178.

A short account with mention of some of the chariots.

V

1513, April 11. Procession for the « Possesso » of Pope Leo X.

Apparently the most magnificent papal *possesso* of the Renaissance, with an extremely long and elaborate procession and many remarkable street decorations. The latter are well documented by verbal descriptions, and a few drawings may survive (see Egger and Frommel, below). The procession went from Saint Peter's to the cathedral of Saint John-in-Lateran via the Ponte Sant'Angelo and the « via papale », passing the Campidoglio and the Colosseum. At Saint John's and in the Lateran Palace there were religious ceremonies and a lavish banquet. In the evening the return to Castel Sant'Angelo was by way of Piazza Giudea, Campo de' Fiori, and Via Florida. Street decorations included both the display of tapestries and ancient statues and the construction of numerous temporary *apparati*. Among the most interesting of the latter: an arch at the Ponte Sant'Angelo commissioned by the commander of the Castello depicting, among other things, Apollo and the Muses and the consignment of the Keys of the Church to Saint Peter; an arch of the Florentine colony in Rome depicting Saint John the Baptist and the Medici patrons Saints Cosma and Damianus; an arch of the *zecchiere* Johann Zink with allusions to the Lateran Council; one commissioned by the banker Agostino Chigi with a famous epigram about Popes Alexander VI, Julius II, and Leo X; one done for the Sauli family with a boy who recited verses. Numerous inscriptions from the *apparati* are recorded. In general the authorship of the *apparati* is unknown, but it is thought by Cruciani, Egger, and Frommel, below, that Baldassare Peruzzi may have worked on at least one arch. It seems not unlikely that Raphael and most other reputable artists residing in the city may have contributed.

Sources

1. Anonymous, *La Coronation du pape Leon X de ce nom faitte a Rome le xi jour d'avril l'an mil cinq cens et treize. Pompe et ordre faicte a l'alee du pape de puis le palais Saint Pierre jusques a Saint Jehan de Lateran le xi jour avril mil CCCCC*

et XIII pour la coronation. N.p., n.d., but probably Paris or Lyons 1513, 4°, cc. 4. Bibliothèque de l'Arsenal, Paris: Fonds Rondel Ra[5]. 910.

Includes a brief account of the cortège with some short descriptions of *apparati.*

2. GRASSI, relevant passages from his diary, printed in CANCELLIERI, *Possessi*, pp. 60-66.

By the papal master of ceremonies, an account interesting mainly for information on preparations for the procession and on the author's dealing with questions of propriety and precedence.

3. GUICCIARDINI, *Storia d'Italia*, vol. III, pp. 259-260.

Some information on the procession, which the author may have witnessed.

4. PENNI, GIAN GIACOMO, *Cronica delle magnifiche et honorate pompe fatte in Roma per la creatione et incoronatione di Papa Leone. X. Pont. Opt. Max.* N.p., n.d., but probably Rome or Florence 1513, 16°, cc. A1-F8. Reprinted entirely in ROSCOE, *Vita e pontificato di Leon X*, vol. V, pp. 189-231, and partially in CANCELLIERI, *Possessi*, pp. 67-84. Edited by Giovanni Rosini as *Narrazione delle pompe fatte in Roma per la creazione di Papa Leon X*, Pisa, Tip. Nistri 1846.

A very good descriptive account in prose in the form of a letter to Contessina de' Medici, the pope's sister, by a Florentine physician residing in Rome. A handsome woodcut on frontispiece shows Leo X riding in the procession. There are an account of the coronation in Saint Peter's that had taken place on March 19 and a description of the April 11 procession, with attention to the *apparati*. Some inscriptions are recorded. Though the work is an early example of a nearly official account, or *livret*, it is written in an informal style, with several passages of self-deprecating humor.

5. SANUDO, *Diarii*, vol. XVI, cols. 160-166 and 678-690.

Two long and rather detailed accounts of the occasion that had been sent to Venice, with some additional particulars supplied by Sanudo. The second account is affected in tone, with many pedantic uses of Latin phrases, but contains perhaps the best descriptions of the *apparati*.

6. TEDALLINI, *Diario romano*, p. 340.

A short, enthusiastic account, with some information on the *apparati*.

Studies

7. CANCELLIERI, *Possessi*, pp. 60-84.

Long quotations from Grassi, from Paolo Giovio's *Vita Leonis X*, from the diary of Sebastiano de' Tebaldini, and from Penni, with many explanatory notes.

8. CRUCIANI, FABRIZIO, *Gli allestamenti scenici di Baldassarre Peruzzi*. « Bollettino del Centro Internazionale di Studi di Architettura Andrea Palladio », vol. XVI, 1974, pp. 156-157.

Suggests, after Egger, below, that Peruzzi may have done an arch for the *possesso*.

9. EGGER, *Entwürfe Baldassare Peruzzis*, pp. 19-20.

Suggests that a drawing in the Siena sketchbook attributed to Peruzzi may represent the arch commissioned by Agostino Chigi for the *possesso*.

10. FROMMEL, *Baldassare Peruzzi als Maler und Zeichner*, pp. 75-76 and figures xxii c and xxii d.

Publishes two drawings from the Uffizi Gallery and the British Museum that he thinks may represent *apparati* for the *possesso*. The second may show the arch commissioned by the Sauli.

11. FIORANI, *Riti ceremonie feste*, pp. 136-140.

A good general account.

12. PASTOR, *Storia dei papi*, vol. IV, parte I, pp. 23-28.

An excellent general account based on all the important sources. Numerous bibliographical references.

13. RODOCANACHI, *Le Pontificat de Léon X*, pp. 41-47.

A very good summary of the celebrations.

14. ROSCOE, *Vita e pontificato di Leon X*, vol. IV, pp. 19-23, and vol. V, pp. 189-231.

A good summary of the occasion and a complete printing of Penni's account. The texts of inscriptions on the *apparati* are supplied in the notes by Roscoe's Italian editor.

VI

1513, September 13-18. FESTIVITIES FOR THE GRANTING OF ROMAN CITIZENSHIP TO GIULIANO AND LORENZO DE' MEDICI, BROTHER AND NEPHEW OF POPE LEO X, JOINED TO AN OUT-OF-SEASON CELEBRATION OF THE ROMAN PATRIOTIC FESTIVAL OF THE « PALILIA ».

A festival remarkable for its themes of « native » Roman classical revival, and one almost unique in the period for the wealth of its surviving literary material. The two young Medici were granted honorary Roman citizenship by the Roman city government, or *comune*, as a gesture of good will toward Pope Leo X, then at the peak of his local popularity. It was this government that commissioned all the works of art and the dramatic productions. It had constructed on the Campidoglio, the city's civic center, an enormous temporary theatre, decorated with numerous paintings in *chiaroscuro*, sculptures and Latin inscriptions. The architect of the theatre is said by Altieri to have been Pietro Rosselli. (See, however, Bruschi, below.) Baldassare Peruzzi is said to have done a painting of Tarpeia and the stage setting for the comedy. The planner of the decorations was the Roman humanist Tommaso Inghirami. The paintings evoked relations between the ancient Romans and the Etruscans (ancestors of the Florentines), as well as famous episodes in Roman legend and history, particularly those associated with the Capitolium. September 13: procession of Giuliano with a large suite from the Vatican to the Campidoglio. (Lorenzo was away in Florence). In the theatre took place a solemn mass, Latin orations by city officials, and a sumptuous banquet (whose courses are recorded). There was a presentation of dramatic skits planned by Camillo Porzio, like Inghirami a member of the Accademia Romana, with the roles played by boys of patrician families. The skits included: (1) an oration by a character representing the Dea Roma; (2) a Latin eclogue featuring yokels from the Roman countryside, with numerous topical references, written by Blosio Palladio; (3) a recitation by a character representing the Deus Capitolinus (verses both composed and spoken by Lorenzo Grana); (4) an appearance of Roma with the allegorical characters of Justice and Fortitude, all reciting verses written by Vincenzo Pimpinella; and (5) the appearance of characters representing the goddess Cybele and the cities of Rome and Florence, with the latter two disputing the possession of Giuliano and Cybele reconciling them (verses by Camillo Porzio). September 14: presentation of the last skit, which featured the dead Clarice Orsini de' Medici, mother of the pope and of Giuliano, with the rivers Tiber and Arno (verses by Maddaleni Capodiferro). Then, as the last and principal element of the entertainments, a playing in Latin of Plautus' comedy *Poenulus* by Roman boys under the direction of Inghirami. September 18: apparent repetition of all the skits and the *Poenulus* before the pope at the Vatican. Of the works of art, only drawings of the theatre's plans seem to survive. (See Ashby, Bruschi, and Cruciani, below). All the inscriptions and all the recited verses are, however, preserved, and there are excellent descriptions both of the decorations and of the performances.

Sources

1. ALTIERI, MARCANTONIO, *Giuliano de' Medici eletto cittadino romano ovvero il Natale di Roma nel 1513, relazione inedita di Marcantonio Altieri*, con prefazione e note di Loreto Pasqualucci. Roma, Altero 1881, pp. 78. Also printed, with corrections, in Cruciani, below, pp. 1-20.

A proud and careful account by a native Roman patrician who was one of the eight planners of the celebration, in the form of a letter to Renzo di Cere, an Orsini. Good descriptions of the theatre and its decorations, a good account of the banquet, and less full relations of the pageant and of the playing of the comedy. Particularly interesting for information about the city government's preparations. Numerous historical notes by the editor. A major source.

2. BENRICEVUTI DA PRATO, ANTONIO, *Lo spectaculo degnissimo del M. Iuliano de Medici fatoli dal P.R. con tutte sue storie ed adornamenti in terza rima.* N.p., n.d. Biblioteca Moreniana, Rome.

Not seen. Described by Cruciani, below, p. xli, as having no information not found in Altieri or Sereno, here listed, on which accounts it is probably dependent.

3. CHIERIGATO, FRANCESCO, a ms. letter to Isabella d'Este quoted at length in CREIGHTON, *History of the Papacy*, vol. IV, pp. 196-197, and in Cruciani, below, p. xlviii.

A complete list of inscriptions (quoted in Creighton only) and much attention to details of the theatrical presentations.

4. NOTTURNO NAPOLETANO (ANTONIO CARACCIOLO), *Triomphi di gli mirandi spettaculi et ricche vivande del solenne convivio fatta da sacri romani al Magnifico Iuliano et Invicto Laurentio de Medici con il resto creato il Sommo Pontefice Leon Decimo con tutta la geonologia et gloria de Firenze e Roma, composti per Nocturno Neapolitano.* Bologna, Hieronymo di Beneditti 1519. Biblioteca Comunale dell'Archiginnasio, Bologna.

Not seen. Described by Cruciani, below, pp. li and xli-xlii, as a versified adaptation of Palliolo's account in Italian prose.

5. PALLIOLO, PAOLO, *Le feste pel conferimento del patriziato romano a Giuliano e Lorenzo de' Medici, narrate da Paolo Palliolo fanese*, ed. O. Guerrini. Bologna, Romagnoli 1885, pp. 160. Printed also in Cruciani, below, pp. 21-67.

Written by a Roman magistrate and addressed to Lucrezia Zanchini, wife of the Senator of Rome, Giacomo Bovio. Perhaps the most informative single account, with good descriptions of the theatre decorations, the recording of many inscriptions, a detailed list of the banquet courses, and careful narration of the pageant, with Italian paraphrases of the verses recited.

6. [PALLIOLO, PAOLO], *Omnium actorum recitatorum in Capitolio quum Magnificus Iulianus Medices romana civitate donatus fuit descriptio*. Ms. published by Cruciani, below, pp. 69-94.

Addressed to the Roman Senator Giacomo Bovio, this account is precious for its complete text of the Latin recitations of the pageant.

7. SANUDO, *Diarii*, vol. XVII, cols. 73-74.

A letter from the Venetian envoy Vetor Lippomano giving a short summary of events, with attention to a dispute over precedence and to the cost of the celebrations.

8. SERENO, AURELIO, *Theatrum capitolinum Magnifico Iuliano institutum per Aurelium Serenum monopolitanum et de elephante carmen eiusdem*. Romae, in aedibus Mazochianis 1514. This original publication not seen. Reprinted in large part, with an Italian translation, by Cruciani, below, pp. 95-123.

A poem in hexameters with rather full description of the pageant and some reporting of recited verses. (The ode at the end of the original publication is dedicated to Hanno, the famous white elephant given to Leo X by the king of Portugal).

9. SICULO, GIULIO SIMONE, *Epulum populi romani eucharisticon per Siculum*. Romae, per Magistrum Stephanum et Magistrum Herculem Socios 1513.

Not seen. Described by Cruciani, below, p. xliv, as a pretentious poem of four hundred hexameters printed only four days after the festival and thus written mostly before the event. This mediocre literary creation was given a sarcastic « scholarly » commentary by Roman letterati. See also Gnoli, below, pp. 103-106.

10. TEDALLINI, *Diario romano*, p. 346.

A short, enthusiastic report of the festivities.

11. VASARI, in his life of Baldassare Peruzzi, *Opere*, vol. IV, pp. 595-596.

States that Peruzzi did the painting of Tarpeia and the stage setting for the comedy.

12. ASHBY, T., JR., *Sixteenth Century Drawings of Roman Buildings Attributed to Andreas Coner*. « Papers of the British School at Rome », vol. II, 1904, p. 23 and illustration 23.

Reproduces contemporary drawings of the theatre's plan, without identifying them.

13. ASHBY, T., JR., *Addenda and Corrigenda to Sixteenth Century Drawings of Roman Buildings Attributed to Andreas Coner*. « Papers of the British School at Rome », vol. VI, 1914, pp. 194-197.

Identifies the drawings of the theatre's plan previously published and compares them to descriptions of the theatre in contemporary accounts.

14. BRUSCHI, ARNALDO, *Il teatro capitolino del 1513*. « Bollettino del Centro Internazionale di Studi di Architettura Andrea Palladio », vol. XVI, 1974, pp. 189-218.

Returning to the subject after his essay in the book of Cruciani, below, the author speculates in more detail on the form of the theatre and intentions of its designers. He publishes again two of the original Coner drawings and suggests that the architect Rosselli may have been carrying out plans made by Giuliano da San Gallo, with, perhaps, the participation of Baldassare Peruzzi.

15. CRUCIANI, FABRIZIO, *Il teatro del Campidoglio e le feste romane del 1513, con la ricostruzione architettonica del teatro di Arnaldo Bruschi*. Milano, Il Polifilo 1968 (« Archivio del teatro italiano », 2), pp. xcvi-167.

Reproductions of contemporary accounts in Italian by Marcantonio Altieri and Paolo Palliolo, and of Latin accounts by Aurelio Sereno and the same Palliolo (the last being published for the first time). Reproduction also of two sixteenth-century drawings of the plan of the theatre attributed to Andreas Coner. Four drawings by Bruschi to show the probable construction of the theatre and the placement of the decorations. Cruciani's introduction includes mention and evaluation of numerous other, less important sixteenth-century sources, places this *festa* in context of the history of Roman and Italian pageantry, drama, and literature, describes the political circumstances of the occasion, gives information on all the known participants, provides an account of the preparations and a summary of all the festive events. The many notes contain a wealth of bibliographical and historical information. This book is a model of festival scholarship and one of the very few nearly definitive studies for our period.

16. D'ANCONA, *Origini del teatro italiano*, vol. II, pp. 84-87.

A short but very good study of the dramatic presentations, based on Altieri and Palliolo.

17. *Enciclopedia dello spettacolo*, under « Roma », vol. VIII, cols. 1111-1112.

A summary of the entertainments, with attention to the form of the theatre.

18. GNOLI, DOMENICO, *Il teatro capitolino del 1513*. In his *La Roma di Leon X*, pp. 83-107.

A very good detailed account of the festivities, with attention to the role of the Campidoglio government and to the context of Roman political and cultural history. Much information on the letterati who planned the dramatic entertainments.

19. JANITSCHEK, HUBERT, *Das Capitolinische Theater vom Jahre 1513: ein Beitrag zur Geschichte des Festwesens der Renaissance*. « Repertorium fur Kunstwissenschaft », Band V, 1882, pp. 259-270.

A very good early study of the theatre's decorations based on the Italian accounts of Altieri and Palliolo and the Latin one of Sereno.

20. LANCIANI, *Storia degli scavi di Roma*, vol. I, pp. 160-161.

A little information from archive sources on the clearing of an area on the Campidoglio for the construction of the theatre.

21. MITCHELL, *Les Intermèdes au service de l'Etat*, pp. 124-127.

A short study of the political content of the dramatic skits.

22. MITCHELL, BONNER, *Rome in the High Renaissance: the Age of Leo X*. Norman, Oklahoma, University of Oklahoma Press 1973 (« The Centers of Civilization », 33), pp. 61-74.

A summary of the celebrations with attention to the themes of classical revival.

23. NEIIENDAM, KLAUS, *Le Théâtre de la Renaissance en Italie*. « Analecta Romana Instituti Danici », vol. V, 1969, pp. 117-120 and 142-154.

The author, who had not seen the study of Cruciani but knew nearly all the sources, examines the 1513 festival in considerable detail, giving much information on the historical background, and speculates on the nature of the stage setting for the comedy.

24. PASTOR, *Storia dei papi*, vol. IV, parte I, pp. 392-393.

A good short summary based on many sources.

25. RODOCANACHI, *Le Pontificat de Léon X*, pp. 65-66.

A short account.

26. ZORZI, *Il teatro e la città*, pp. 98 and 198 (note).

A short discussion of the theatre.

1536, April 5-18. ENTRY AND SOJOURN OF THE EMPEROR CHARLES V, DURING A TRIUMPHAL PROGRESS UP THE PENINSULA AFTER THE VICTORY OF TUNIS.

For students of classical revival, this entry into Rome as a victorious *imperator* is the most poignant of all Charles V's numerous triumphal entries. Arriving from Naples, he came by the Via Appia Antica and the Porta San Sebastiano (ancient Porta Capuana). The procession went along the route of the ancient Via Triumphalis, much of which had been newly cleared, at great expense, for the occasion, past the Baths of Caracalla, the Arch of Constantine, the Colosseum, the Arch of Titus, the Arch of Septimius Severus, the Piazza San Marco, the Campidoglio, and the Ponte Sant'Angelo to Saint Peter's, where the emperor was awaited by Pope Paul III. The Conservatori of the city government walked alongside Charles' horse, pointing out to him the principal ancient monuments, which, in combination with the special *apparati*, created a matchless triumphal setting. The three most important *apparati* were: (1) a triumphal arch at the Porta San Sebastiano with sculpture and paintings evoking scenes of Roman history or legend; (2) an enormous temporary triumphal arch at Piazza San Marco, with statues and paintings representing Holy Roman Emperors of the Habsburg family and scenes of Charles' own life; (3) on the Ponte Sant'Angelo, statues of Saints Peter and Paul, the four evangelists, and four Old Testament fathers; and (4) *apparati* in the Piazza di San Pietro and at the door of the Vatican Palace showing, among other things, Saint Peter and Saint Paul and the Emperors Augustus and Constantine. Artists known to have worked on the entry *apparati*: Antonio da San Gallo (the arch at San Marco), Raffaello da Montelupo, Francesco Salviati, Ermanno Fiammingo, Francesco Maso (« l'Indaco »), Girolamo Pilotto, Vittorio Alessandrino, Giovanni da Castel Bolognese, Battista Franco, Sandrino, and a Martino Tedesco. It no longer seems likely that Baldassare Peruzzi (who died several months before the entry) had anything to do with the planning or that the Dutchman Martin van Heemskerck can be identified with « Martino

Tedesco ». (See the studies by De Angelis D'Ossat, Egger, and Toca, below). A few drawings seem to survive. (See Giovannoni and Toca, below).

Studies

1. ALBERINI, MARCELLO, *Il diario di Marcello Alberini (1521-1536)*, ed. Domenico Oriani. « Archivio della R. Società Romana di Storia Patria », vol. XIX, 1896, pp. 43-49.

A fragment from a Roman's book of recollections dealing in great detail with the clearing of the Via Triumphalis and, quite briefly, with the temporary arch constructed at San Marco. Excellent notes by the editor.

2. CEFFINO, ZANOBIO, *La triomphante entrata di Carlo V. imperadore augusto in l'alma citta di Roma con il significato delli archi triumphali et delle figure antiche in prosa e versi latini*. N.p., n.d., but probably Rome 1536, 4°, cc. 4. Biblioteca Statale, Lucca: Bte CC XXXIII. 19. Bibliothèque Nationale, Paris: Rés. Oc. 1815. Appeared also in French, Flemish, and German translations.

An excellent systematic account in the form of a letter to Alessandro de' Medici, duke of Florence, dated April 6, 1536. Good description of the *apparati*, with the text of their inscriptions. The author has more information than Sala, below, on decorations at the Castel Sant'Angelo, in the Borgo, and at Saint Peter's and the Vatican. A major source.

3. MARTINELLI, BIAGIO (BIAGIO DA CESENA), relevant passages from his ms. diary published by Podestà, below.

Much information about the entry and later activities of Charles V, from the point of view of the papal master of ceremonies. Little attention to the *apparati*.

4. RABELAIS, FRANÇOIS, letters to Bishop Geoffroy d'Estissac dated from Rome December 30, 1535, January 28 and February 15, 1536. In *Oeuvres complètes*, ed. Pierre Jourda, Paris, Garnier 1963, vol. II, pp. 533-559.

Describes the feverish preparations for the emperor's visit, particularly the clearing of the Via Triumphalis.

5. [SALA, ANDREA], an account of the Roman entry in his *Ordine pompe apparati et ceremonie, delle solenne intrate di Carlo. V. Imp. sempre Aug. nella città di Roma,. Siena, et Fiorenza*, cc. A2r-B3v. Also published separately, Rome, [A. Blado] 1536: British Museum, London: 1057 h 9 (6). Reprinted in FORCELLA, *Tornei e giostre*, pp. 39-50.

A systematic, semi-official report, with a careful account of the procession, good descriptions of the *apparati*, and recording of inscriptions. The main source.

6. SANTA CRUZ, *Crónica del Emperador Carlos V*, vol. III, pp. 322-352.

By the emperor's would-be Spanish historiographer, who must have used explicit contemporary documents, a very detailed account of the entry and of later events during Charles' stay, with considerable description of the *apparati*, explanation of their mythological and historical allusions, and some inscriptions in Spanish translation.

7. VANDENESSE, *Journal des voyages de Charles-Quint*, pp. 117-131.

By a member of the emperor's household, an account with some information on the procession and much about the Easter mass in Saint Peter's, but nothing about the *apparati*.

8. VASARI, in the lives of Francesco Maso (l'Indaco), Raffaello da Montelupo, Antonio da San Gallo, Battista Franco, and Francesco Salviati, *Opere*, vol. III, p. 682; vol. IV, p. 545; vol. V, pp. 464-465; vol. VI, pp. 571-573; and vol. VII, p. 15.

A great deal of close second-hand information about the *apparati*, doubtless derived in large part from Raffaello da Montelupo, who hurried on to Florence to work on decorations there.

Studies

9. CANCELLIERI, *Storia de' solenni possessi*, pp. 93-102.

Reprints Sala's account with lengthy notes that are particularly informative about the route of the procession.

10. CHASTEL, *Les Entrées de Charles-Quint en Italie*, pp. 199-201.

A careful analysis of the *apparati*, based mainly on Vasari, with information about the artists who worked on them.

11. DE ANGELIS D'OSSAT, GUGLIELMO, *Gli archi trionfali ideati dal Peruzzi per la venuta a Roma di Carlo V*. « Capitolium », anno XVIII, 1943, pp. 287-294.

Taking as his point of departure Egger's essay, below, the author argues that some drawings in the Siena Sketchbook, long attributed to Peruzzi, are in fact copies from him and that they represent unexecuted designs for *apparati* in the emperor's entry. (This opinion is contested by Toca, below.) Reproduction of six of the sketches, with attempted identification of the proposed locations of the *apparati*.

12. DOREZ, LEON, *La Cour du Pape Paul III, d'après les régistres de la trésorerie secrète*, Paris, Ernest Leroux 1932, tome I, pp. 250-268.

A good account of the negotiations and preparations preceding the entry, based largely on ms. material, and some information on events during the emperor's stay. Little on the entry itself.

13. Egger, *Entwürfe Baldassare Peruzzis für den Einzüg Karls V in Rom*, pp. 1-44.

Argues that Peruzzi must have participated in the planning of the *apparati* before his death in January, 1536. Associates seven drawings in the so-called Peruzzi Sketchbook of Siena with plans for the decoration of Porta San Sebastiano and for the arch at San Marco, while concluding that they are poor copies made by an art student from Peruzzi's originals.

14. Egger, Hermann, *Zur Dauer von Martens van Heemskerck Aufenhalt in Rom (1532-1535)*. « Mededeelingen van het Nederlandsch Historisch Instituut te Rome », Deel V, 1925, pp. 119-127.

Shows that Heemskerck was not in Rome after the summer of 1535 and thus that (as he had already argued in an earlier study) that artist cannot be identified with the « Martino Tedesco » who Vasari says worked on the entry *apparati*.

15. Fiorani, *Riti ceremonie feste*, pp. 144-147.

A good short account, with special attention to the preparations for the clearing of the Via Triumphalis.

16. Forcella, *Tornei e giostre*, pp. 35-50.

Reprints Sala's account with a short introduction about the artists who worked on the *apparati*.

17. Giovannoni, Gustavo, *Antonio San Gallo il giovane*, Roma, Tip. Regionale 1959, vol. I, pp. 309-312; and vol. II, figs. 327-331.

Discusses San Gallo's work on the *apparati* and reproduces four drawings of that artist now at the Uffizi that have to do with them. Reproduces as well another drawing apparently connected with the *apparati* which he hesitantly attributes to Peruzzi.

18. Jacquot, *Panorama des fêtes et cérémonies du règne*, p. 431.

A short but valuable analysis of the *apparati*, based on several sources.

19. Lanciani, *Storia degli scavi di Roma*, vol. II, pp. 48-63.

A great deal of information on the demolitions and digging carried out to clear the way of the Via Triumphalis. Based on material in the city archives.

20. Pastor, *Storia dei papi*, vol. V, pp. 159-167.

A good account of the entry and of other events during the emperor's stay with, however, little attention to the *apparati*.

21. Podesta, B., *Carlo Quinto a Roma nell'anno 1536*. « Archivio della R. Società Romana di Storia Patria », vol. I, 1877-78, pp. 303-344.

Publishes the relevant passages from the diary of Biagio Martinelli, papal master of ceremonies, and a number of entries from archival account books showing payments to artists who worked on the decorations. Provides excellent explanatory notes for the passages from Martinelli. A very valuable early study.

22. STRONG, *Splendour at Court*, pp. 94-95.

A short analysis of the *apparati* with reproduction of two drawings from the so-called Peruzzi Sketchbook of Siena (see De Angelis, Egger, and Toca, here listed) which seem to show the Porta San Sebastiano and the arch at San Marco.

23. TOCA, MIRCEA, *Osservazioni sul cosidetto taccuino senese di Baldassare Peruzzi*. « Annali della Scuola Normale Superiore di Pisa, classe di lettere e filosofia », serie III, vol. I, parte I, 1971, pp. 161-179.

Argues that the Siena Sketchbook is not of Peruzzi's hand, that that artist did not participate in the planning of the entry, and that the drawings of *apparati* in the book are by Jacomo Melighino, who did them not from originals by Peruzzi but from the completed *apparati* themselves.

VIII

1538, July 24. TRIUMPHAL ENTRY OF POPE PAUL III ON HIS RETURN FROM A CONFERENCE HELD IN NICE TO MAKE PEACE BETWEEN KING FRANCIS I OF FRANCE AND THE EMPEROR CHARLES V.

The city officials went out in an elaborate procession to greet the pope at Ponte Molle. He entered the city by the Porta del Popolo, paused in the church of Santa Maria del Popolo, then proceeded by way of the Castel Sant'Angelo and the church of Sant'Ambrogio to the Palazzo San Marco, his temporary residence. Principal *apparati*: a triumphal arch at the Porta del Popolo, decorations of the facade of Sant'Ambrogio, special temporary decoration of an ancient arch called the Arco di Portogallo (now demolished), and an unfinished arch at San Marco. Theme of the decorations: the pope as peacemaker and as founder of a new alliance against the Turks. Apparently no drawings survive and the artists are unknown.

Source

1. DANZA, PAOLO, *La gloriosa e solenne intrata della S.N.S. Papa Paulo III in Roma dopo il santo viaggio di Nizza, archi triomphali e statue fatte da li romani con i loro titoli e significati* [...]. N.p., no pub., 1538, 8°, cc. 8, of which the first

five are relevant. Biblioteca Apostolica Vaticana, Rome: Racc. I, VI. 340, int. 4. Published also from a ms. copy by FORCELLA, *Tornei e giostre*, pp. 53-62.

A very carefully done account with a meticulous list of the procession, good descriptions of the *apparati*, and recording of the inscriptions.

2. SANTA CRUZ, *Crónica del Emperador Carlos V*, vol. III, pp. 517-518.

The author, who was probably not present but must have seen contemporary documents, mentions several of the *apparati* and gives some inscriptions in Spanish translation.

Studies

3. PASTOR, *Storia dei papi*, vol. V, p. 193.

A brief account of the pope's return to Rome.

4. PECCHIAI, *Roma nel Cinquecento*, p. 64.

States that the expenses of the entry *apparati* bore heavily on the city government and refers to documents in the archives of the Campidoglio.

IX

1549, March 4. TOURNAMENT AND OTHER GAMES HELD BY THE FRENCH AMBASSADOR CARDINAL JEAN DU BELLAY TO CELEBRATE THE BIRTH OF LOUIS, SECOND SON OF KING HENRY II.

An interesting, well-documented example of celebrations held by a foreign colony in Rome. Both a naumachia and a sciomachia were planned, but the former was made impossible by a flood of the Tiber. The sciomachia was held in the Piazza dei Santi Apostoli, where an enormous temporary castle had been constructed. There is no record of special *apparati* with civic themes, but the narration of the tournament, which included elaborate chivalric ceremonies, dramatic presentations, comic performances, and music, is detailed. Orazio Farnese, a grandson of Pope Paul III, was the most prominent participant.

Sources

1. COLEINE, COLA, a passage from his ms. diary published in FORCELLA, *Tornei e giostre*, pp. 115-116, and in CLEMENTI, *Carnevale romano*, pp. 203-204.

A short account, with attention to individual jousts.

2. RABELAIS, FRANÇOIS, *La Sciomachie et festins faits a Rome au palais de Mon Seigneur Reverendissime Cardinal Du Bellay pour l'heureuse naissance de Mon Seigneur d'Orleans, le tout extrait d'une copie des lettres ecrites a Mon Seigneur le Reverendissime Cardinal de Guise par M. Francois Rabelais, docteur en medicine.* Lyon, Sebastien Gryph 1549, 4°, pp. 31. Reprinted in Rabelais' *Oeuvres complètes*, ed. Pierre Jourda, Paris, Garnier 1963, vol. II, pp. 579-599.

An excellent careful account from which nearly all our information comes. No mention of artistic *apparati* or of inscriptions.

Study

3. PASTOR, *Storia dei papi*, vol. V, pp. 234-235.

A short evocation of the occasion, with archival references.

X

1550, February 18. CELEBRATION BY THE ROMAN CITY GOVERNMENT FOR THE ELECTION OF POPE JULIUS III, A ROMAN.

A temporary theatre was constructed in the courtyard of the Palazzo dei Conservatori, on the Campidoglio. Inside there were twelve paintings, with inscriptions, whose theme was parallels between the new pope and Julius Caesar. The artists are apparently unknown. After a banquet in the theatre there was a performance of an unidentified comedy, set in Modena, with a special prologue in praise of the pope.

Source

1. ANONYMOUS, *Triomphale festa delli Sig.ri romani per la creatione di P. Iulio III.* Biblioteca Casanatense, Rome.

Not seen. Cited by Clementi, below.

2. CLEMENTI, *Carnevale romano*, pp. 206-208.

Using as sources the ms. diary of Cola Coleine and the anonymous *Triomphale festa*, the author reconstructs the celebrations.

3. PASTOR, *Storia dei papi*, vol. VI, p. 45.

A mention of the celebrations with a reference to a ms. source.

SAVONA

I

1507, June 27-July 1. Meeting of King Louis XII of France, Coming from Milan, and King Ferdinand of Aragon, Returning to Spain from a Visit to the Kingdom of Naples.

A « summit meeting » interesting for its elaborate ceremonies and for the extreme courtesy with which the two kings treated each other. Savona was then in Louis' possessions. He had a special pier constructed for the landing of Ferdinand and his queen, Germaine de Foix, Louis' relative. After ceremonies of greeting, and a modest dispute over the question of who should go first, the sovereigns rode into the town on mules, the queen riding behind Louis on his mount. The keys of the city were offered to Louis and refused. Street decorations included at least one arch of « verdure ». An inscription is preserved. Ferdinand stayed at the Castello, and Louis at the Bishop's Palace. The meetings of the following days entailed further elaborate ceremonies.

Sources

1. Auton, *Chroniques*, tome IV, pp. 122-149.

By the king's chronicler, who was present, a very detailed account of events with much attention to the two monarchs' courtesies to each other. Mention of some *apparati* and of an inscription.

2. Guicciardini, *Storia d'Italia*, vol. II, pp. 208-213.

A good summary of events and of the elaborate courtesies with which the two sovereigns treated each other.

3. Santa Cruz, Alonso De, *Crónica de los reyes católicos (hasta ahora iné-dita)*, edición y estudio por Juan de Mata Carriazo. Sevilla, Escuela de Estudios Hispano-Americanos 1951, tomo II, p. 95.

A very short account.

Studies

4. Lippi, Giovanni, *Il convegno in Savona tra Luigi XII e Ferdinando il Cat-tolico.* « Atti e Memorie della Società Storica Savonese », vol. II, 1889-90, pp. 1-40.

A very good account of the occasion based on d'Auton and several ms. sources. Gives the text of one welcoming inscription and publishes copies of privileges granted to the city by the two kings.

5. Maulde de La Clavière, R. de, *L'Entrevue de Savone en 1507.* « Revue d'Histoire Diplomatique », année IV, 1890, pp. 583-590.

Summarizes in some detail the elaborate ceremonies and arrangements for the meeting, drawing mainly on d'Auton but also on a number of ms. sources. Settles the question of the agreements reached by the two sovereigns by publishing the text of an oath sworn by Louis XII.

SIENA

I

1494, December 2. ENTRY OF KING CHARLES VIII OF FRANCE ON HIS
WAY TO THE CONQUEST OF THE KINGDOM OF NAPLES.

Entry by the Porta Camollia and procession under a *baldacchino*
to the Bishop's Palace, where the king stayed. *Apparati*: an arch
at the Porta Camollia representing Siena as the city of the Virgin;
at least one other triumphal arch at an inner gate with representations
of Charlemagne and Charles VIII himself. Inscriptions on these *apparati* and on the door of the palace are preserved, as are Latin verses
sung to the king, in the name of the Virgin, on his arrival at the palace. Woodcuts in the early ed. of the *Vergier d'honneur*, below, seem
to evoke the *apparati*. Names of artists unknown.

Sources

1. DESREY, *Relation du voyage du Roy Charles VIII*, in Godefroy ed., p. 205;
in Cimber ed., pp. 221-222.

A short report of the king's entry and stay.

2. LA VIGNE, *Vergier d'honneur*, ca. 1500 ed., cc. h2v-h4v; *Histoire du voyage
de Naples*, p. 120; *La Très Curieuse et Chevaleresque Hystoire de la conqueste de
Naples*, pp. 47-51.

Short accounts of the entry with rather general references to the *apparati*, passing
note of the recited verses, and the text of some inscriptions. The early ed. of the *Vergier
d'honneur* has four woodcuts that may allude freely to the *apparati*.

3. SANUDO, *La spedizione di Carlo VIII in Italia*, pp. 144-147.

A short account with, however, considerable description of the *apparati*, the
texts of five inscriptions and that of the sung verses. The main source.

4. CHERRIER, *Histoire de Charles VIII*, tome II, pp. 50-54.

A good summary of the entry with considerable attention to the *apparati*.

5. DELABORDE, *L'Expédition de Charles VIII en Italie*, p. 490.

A good summary with some description of the *apparati*.

6. PECCI, *Memorie storiche-critiche*, vol. I, pp. 94-111.

Little information about the *apparati* and no recording of inscriptions, but much about political negotiations during the king's stay. The author quotes numerous minor sources, both printed and manuscript.

7. PROVEDI, *Relazioni delle pubbliche feste date in Siena*, pp. 35-37.

A good short accourt based on La Vigne and two ms. chronicles.

II

1536, April 23-28. ENTRY AND SOJOURN OF THE EMPEROR CHARLES V DURING HIS TRIUMPHAL PROGRESS UP THE PENINSULA AFTER THE VICTORY OF TUNIS.

Entry of the emperor and his courtiers (without the army) by the Porta Nuova, where he was greeted by city officials and one hundred specially costumed youths. Procession under a *baldacchino* to the Piazza dello Spediale and the Duomo, which the emperor entered for devotions, then on to the Palazzo Petrucci, where he was to stay. Later visit by the Signoria, to the emperor in his palace, and a visit from him to them in the Palazzo Pubblico, from which, on April 24, he watched a *gioco de' pugni* in the Campo. The Accademia degli Intronati had rehearsed an original comedy, l'*Amor costante*, by one of its members, Alessandro Piccolomini, but the Signoria, not sure the emperor would stay long enough to see it, had not appropriated money for the stage scenery and the comedy was not played. Principal *apparati* for the entry: (1) a triumphal arch at the city gate with inscriptions and statues of Faith and Charity:

(2) at the Posterla, a large wooden eagle, made for that quarter of the city, with the insinuating inscription « Praesidium Libertatis Nostrae »; at the Piazza dello Spedale, an enormous equestrian statue of the emperor with his horse stamping on three figures that were, according to different sources, either vanquished princes or river gods representing conquered lands. Domenico Beccafumi was the sculptor of the statue. The names of other artists are not known, and no drawings seem to survive.

Sources

1. ANONYMOUS, *Carlo Quinto in Siena nell'aprile del 1536, relazione di un contemporaneo*, pubblicata per cura di Pietro Vigo. Bologna, Romagnoli 1884 (« Scelta di curiosità letterarie inedite o rare dal sec. XIII al XIX », dispensa CXCIX), pp. xxiv-52.

A very careful « descrittione delle cerimonie, pompa et ordine che si tenne per honorare Carlo V » written by one of the city's magistrates. Much on the city's preparations. Good description of the *apparati*, with inscriptions. An excellent historical introduction by the editor. One of the two main sources.

2. [SALA, ANDREA], *La felice entrata dello imperatore in la citta famosa di Siena, con li superbi apparati*, in his *Ordine pompe, apparati*, cc. B4r-C3v.

A very careful account, with good description of the *apparati* and recording of the inscriptions, by the author of the accounts of the entries into Messina, Naples, Rome, and Florence. One of the two main sources.

3. SANTA CRUZ, *Crónica del Emperador Carlos V*, vol. III, pp. 354-355.

A short account by the emperor's would-be Spanish historiographer, who doubtless saw some contemporary documents. Some description of the *apparati*, one inscription in Spanish translation.

4. VANDENESSE, *Journal des voyages de Charles-Quint*, p. 132.

A short recording of the emperor's visit.

5. VASARI, in the life of Domenico Beccafumi, *Opere*, vol. V, pp. 644-645.

States that the equestrian statue of the emperor had been made by Beccafumi for an expected visit in 1530 which did not take place and that it was brought out of storage and erected in the Piazza for the 1536 entry.

6. CHASTEL, *Les Entrées de Charles-Quint en Italie*, pp. 201-202.

Some description of the *apparati*, based on Vasari.

7. JACQUOT, *Panorama des cérémonies et fêtes du règne*, pp. 431-433.

A good analysis of the *apparati*, with interesting speculation on the iconographical details of Beccafumi's equestrian statue.

8. PECCI, *Memorie storico-critiche*, tomo III, pp. 81-91.

A rather full account based on an official record in the Siena Archivio di Stato. Good description of the *apparati*, recordings of inscriptions, narration of the meetings between the emperor and the Signoria.

9. PROVEDI, *Relazione delle pubbliche feste date in Siena*, pp. 39-44.

A good short account based on several printed and ms. sources, with some description of the *apparati* and some inscriptions.

10. STRONG, *Splendour at Court*, p. 95.

A description of Beccafumi's statue.

TRENT

I

1549, January 24-29. ENTRY AND SOJOURN OF PRINCE PHILLIP OF
SPAIN, ON HIS WAY TO AUSTRIA, GERMANY, AND THE LOW COUN-
TRIES.

A very elaborate entry by the Porta di Santa Croce and procession, in the company of Cardinal Madruzzo, prince of Trent (who
had accompanied Phillip from Spain), to the Duomo and Castello.
Principal *apparati*: a triumphal arch at the Porta with arms, a statue
of Neptune, and inscriptions, including Bible verses; five other arches with inscriptions along the way; near the Piazza del Castello,
a colossal statue of Hercules with inscriptions of Spanish verses;
at the Piazza del Castello, an enormous globe with fireworks and
moving parts, topped by a crowned imperial eagle; and over the
door of the Duomo, a figure of the river god Adige, who rose and
recited Spanish verses to the prince. Entertainments during the
prince's stay included jousts and an extremely elaborate attack on
a mock castle, with many actors, complicated machines (one of
which represented Hell), and fireworks displays. No drawings seem
to survive, and the artists are apparently unknown, but there are
good descriptions, and the inscriptions and verses are recorded.

Sources

1. ALVAREZ, *Relación del camino del Principe D. Felipe*, exact reference
unknown.

Not seen. Since this account was done by a member of the prince's party, it may
be an important source.

2. CALVETE, *El felicissimo viaje*, cc. 44v-52v.

A systematic, detailed account by the chronicler of the prince's journey. Description of the *apparati* and the text of inscriptions. The main source.

3. SANTA CRUZ, *Crónica del Emperador Carlos V*, vol. V, pp. 264-266.

Short characterizations of the main entry *apparati* and a good deal of information on later entertainments, including the mock assault on the castle. Perhaps based mainly on Calvete.

4. ULLOA, *Vita e fatti dell'invitissimo Imperatore Carlo V*, cc. 189v-191r.

A good account with description of some of the *apparati* and the texts of some inscriptions. The author may well have been present but probably refreshed his memory by reading Calvete.

Studies

5. D'ANCONA, *Origini del teatro italiano*, vol. II, p. 149 (note).

Mentions a mime, figuring Hercules and Cerberus in Hell, performed during the prince's stay.

6. JACQUOT, *Panorama des fêtes et cérémonies du règne*, pp. 444-445.

An excellent short analysis of the *apparati*.

7. MARIANI, MICHEL'ANGELO, *Trento con il Sacro Concilio et altri notabili* [...] *descrittion' historica libri tre*. Trento, n. pub., 1672, pp. 357-366.

Quite a detailed account, perhaps based on Calvete and some ms. sources. Good description of the *apparati* and the texts of inscriptions and recited Spanish verses. A very interesting narration of the attack on the mock castle.

8. NICOLINI, *Sul viaggio di Filippo d'Asburgo in Italia*, pp. 264-265.

A short summary of events with description of the principal *apparati*, based on the main sources.

9. ZENATTI, ALBINO, *Rappresentazioni sacre nel Trentino*. « Archivio Storico per Trieste, l'Istria, e il Trentino », vol. II, 1883, pp. 193-194.

Quotes Mariani's account of the entertainments on the Piazza del Castello with the assault of the mock castle.

TURIN

I

1494, September 5. ENTRY OF KING CHARLES VIII OF FRANCE, ON HIS WAY TO CONQUER THE KINGDOM OF NAPLES.

The king was greeted by his hostess, the duchess of Savoy. Several *mystères*, in the medieval tradition of French royal entries, were played on platforms erected in the streets. Characters mentioned as having been portrayed include Abraham, Isaac, Lancelot of the Lake, Jason and Hercules. Biblical, chivalric, and mythological themes were thus combined. There were apparently also allusions to Charlemagne and to a visit he had paid to the city. Buffoons accompanied the king's procession.

Sources

1. DESREY, *Relation du voyage du Roy Charles VIII*, in the Godefroy ed., pp. 196-197; in the Cimber ed., pp. 209-210.

Contains rapid but very interesting allusions to various *apparati*. A major source.

2. LA VIGNE, *Vergier d'honneur*, ca. 1500 ed., cc. d4v-d6v; *La Très Curieuse et Chevaleresque Hystoire de la conqueste de Naples*, pp. 21-22.

Some information on the *apparati*, and mention of the subjects of the *mystères*. Paraphrase of one inscription. A major source.

3. SANUDO, *La spedizione di Carlo VIII in Italia*, p. 85.

A brief recording of the king's passage.

Studies

4. BURCKHARDT, *La civiltà del Rinascimento in Italia*, vol. II, p. 169.

In the author's famous chapter on Renaissance festivals, a summary of the *mystères*, based on La Vigne, above.

5. CHARTROU, *Les Entrées solennelles et triomphales à la Renaissance*, p. 74.

A short description of the *apparati*, based on La Vigne, above.

6. CHERRIER, *Histoire de Charles VIII*, tome I, pp. 434-435.

A summary of the entry with some attention to the *apparati*.

7. D'ANCONA, *Origini del teatro italiano*, vol. I, pp. 297-298.

Examines the descriptions given by Desrey and La Vigne of the *mystères* performed on the king's entry.

8. DELABORDE, *L'Expédition de Charles VIII en Italie*, pp. 397-398.

A short account of the king's visit.

9. FERRIERO DI LAURIANO, FRANCESCO MARIA, *Istoria dell'augusta città di Torino*. Torino, Zappata 1712, parte II, p. 494.

A short account with, however, quotations from ms. sources.

10. GABOTTO, FERDINANDO, *Lo stato sabaudo da Amedeo VIII ad Emanuele Filiberto*. Torino e Roma, L. Roux 1892, vol. III, pp. 511-513.

A good short account giving some attention to the *apparati*, with references to the French sources and quotation of a letter briefly reporting the entry addressed to Ludovico il Moro of Milan.

VENICE

I

1495, April 12 (Palm Sunday). PROCESSION IN SAINT MARK'S SQUARE TO CELEBRATE THE FORMATION OF A LEAGUE TO OPPOSE KING CHARLES VIII OF FRANCE.

A curious blending of religious and political themes in the Venetian style. After the government had brought about an alliance with Pope Alexander VI, King Ferdinand of Spain, and Ludovico il Moro of Milan to oppose Charles VIII, then returning up the peninsula after the conquest of Naples, it chose the occasion of an annual Palm Sunday procession to announce the new league. The doge and ambassadors of allied powers heard mass and then reviewed the procession, which passed through Saint Mark's after going around the square. The procession included a number of Venetian *scuole*, some with allegorical chariots or other *apparati*, and several groups of monks and priests, some of the former carrying religious relics. Among the chariots: one with David and Abigail, one with « Italia » and several provinces, and one representing each of the allied states. The latter bore inscriptions, and as each passed before the doge someone recited a rhyming couplet of explanation. After the procession, the doge came out of the church and the league was formally proclaimed in the square. Some inscriptions and verses are recorded.

Sources

1. COMINES, *Mémoires*, tome III, pp. 126-133.

A poignant account of the celebration by the mortified French ambassador. Though Comines declined the cynical Venetian invitation to attend the ceremonies, he was able to perceive some of the *apparati* from his house.

2. MALIPIERO, DOMENICO, *Annali veneti dall'anno 1457 al 1500 del Senatore Domenico Malipiero*, ordinati e abbreviati dal Senatore Francesco Longo con prefazione e annotazioni di Agostino Sagredo. « Archivio Storico Italiano », tomo VII, parte I, 1843, p. 337.

A short account of the procession and ceremonies.

3. SANUDO, *La spedizione di Carlo VIII*, pp. 299-305.

A formal, systematic account that contains most of the surviving information. Includes the texts of some inscriptions and recited verses.

Studies

4. BURCKHARDT, *La civiltà italiana del Rinascimento*, vol. II, pp. 184-185.

In the author's famous chapter on Renaissance festivals, a short but interesting account of the procession based a ms. letter of Marcantonio Sabellico.

5. D'ANCONA, *Origini del teatro italiano*, vol. I, p. 298.

A short account with a quotation of Comines.

6. PORTIOLI, ATTILIO, *La lega contro Carlo VIII nel 1495*. Mantova, Mondovi 1876, pp. 14 (Nozze Dal Vecchio-Norsa).

The author describes the historical background of the alliance and quotes at length a letter addressed to the marquess of Mantua by Antonio Salimbene that contains information complementing that given by Sanudo.

II

1502, July 31-August 22. VISIT OF ANNE DE FOIX, THE NEW QUEEN OF HUNGARY, EN ROUTE TO JOIN HER HUSBAND IN HIS KINGDOM.

The most elaborate example of a state visit to Venice during our period. The queen was fêted in Venetian mainland possessions and then met at San Biagio Catoldo on July 31 by the doge, other members of the government, and foreign ambassadors, in the Bucentaur, and accompanied to her lodgings in the Venetian palace of the duke of Ferrara. On later days she visited the Palazzo Ducale, the Arsenal, and the glass works at Murano, and watched *regate* and a joust held in her honor on the Grand Canal. On August 5 there was a ball in the Palazzo Ducale with nummeries depicting episodes of the Trojan War (e.g. the Judgment of Paris and the Rape of Helen), with extremely elaborate *apparati*. The movements of the mummeries, like those of an earlier joust on the canal, were apparently done in time to music. The queen was enchanted with her visit and, as is plain from Venetian sources, overstayed her welcome, spending a great deal more of the republic's money than it had set aside for her maintenance.

Sources

1. GABRIELI, ANGELO, *Libellus hospitalis munificentiae venetorum in excipienda Anna regina Hungariae*. This original edition not seen. Reprinted with facing Italian translation by Francesco Testa, in *Traduzione di una lettera latina di Angelo Gabrieli stampata l'anno 1502, descrittiva le feste date in Venezia e nello stato veneto ad Anna principessa di Francia, che passava in detto anno a sposare Ladislao re d'Ungheria*. Padova, Tipi della Minerva 1837, pp. 47 (Nozze Negri-Stecchini). Biblioteca Nazionale, Firenze: Palat. Misc. Capretta 473.5.

A formal account by a Venetian senator, and friend of the writer Pietro Bembo, addressed to the Venetian ambassador in Hungary. A considerable amount of information on the queen's reception in Brescia, Vicenza, Padua, and Venice. The author compares her Venetian entry to the ancient Roman triumphs and maintains that a city with canals allows the most majestic sort of reception. Particularly interesting for the account of the queen's arrival in the Bucentaur (surrounded by many small craft), for the description of the regate, and for that of the mummeries played in the doge's palace. Includes the text of a Latin oration delivered to the queen by the author in the name of the senate and that of a Latin ode written by « il nostro Armonio » and set to music by Pietro de' Fossi. The music is not recorded.

2. PRIULI, *Diarii*, vol. II, pp. 218-223.

A considerable amount of information. The author, who apparently had some official function in the reception, takes a less enthusiastic view than that of Gabrieli. The editor's notes refer to some ms. sources.

3. SANUDO, *Diarii*, vol. IV, cols. 287-288, 294-296, 301, and 306-307.

Sanudo had been personally in charge of the queen's reception in Verona, and he gives a very full account of her stay in Venice, with much talk of expenditures.

4. Molmenti, Pompeo Gherardo, *La storia di Venezia nella vita privata dalle origini alla caduta della repubblica*, 4ª ed. interamente rifatta. Bergamo, Istituto Italiano d'Arti Grafiche 1906, vol. II, p. 96.

A short account with a reference to a French ms. description of all receptions offered to the queen on her way to Hungary.

5. Tamassia Mazzarotto, Bianca, *Le feste veneziane: i giochi popolari, le cerimonie religiose e di governo*. Firenze, Sansoni 1961, pp. xvii and 59.

Some information on the entertainments, particularly on a regata of women.

III

1530, January 1. Procession in Saint Mark's Square to Celebrate the « Publication of Peace », or New Alliance of the Emperor, the Pope, Milan, and Venice.

Mass by the Patriarch of Venice in Saint Mark's. A procession around the piazza, in the presence of the doge, of various *scuole* and religious groups. Proclamation of the peace. Carried in the procession were representations of Saint Mark, the pope, the emperor, the King of the Romans Ferdinand, the doge, the duke of Milan, and «Justice». Decoration of the inside of Saint Mark's, but not of the outside because of rainy weather.

Sources

1. Sanudo, Marino, *Della solenne processione fatta in Venezia per la lega conchiusa tra Carlo V imperatore e la repubblica veneta*. Venezia, Antonelli 1852, pp. 18.

Not seen. Probably a publication of the account later to appear in the *Diarii*, below, perhaps with introduction and notes.

2. Sanudo, *Diarii*, vol. LII, cols. 435-437.

The source of nearly all our information on the procession and other ceremonies. The author records the unhappiness of the ambassadors of Florence, France, and England, left out of the alliance.

IV

1530, October 11-November 5. VISIT OF FRANCESCO II SFORZA, DUKE OF MILAN.

The duke, whose recent investiture was owed largely to the friendly support of the Venetian republic, was met at the island of San Clemente on October 11 by the doge and other officials in the Bucentaur and taken to a residence on the Grand Canal. On subsequent days he was received by the doge and the Collegio in the Palazzo Ducale, witnessed a regata and a naumachia on the Grand Canal, and attended a banquet and ball, with mummeries whose content is unknown. In Chioggia, where the duke had embarked for Venice, there had also been « eclogues » and comedies, the nature of which is not known.

Source

1. SANUDO, *Diarii*, vol. LIV, cols. 35-40, 43-45, 48-49, 50-60, 63, 65-67, 69-70, 72, 79-84, 90-91, 93, 97-99, 101. Main passages published also by Contarini, below.

A great deal of information on the ceremonies and entertainments. There is an interesting marginal observation that the Venetians vainly requested a relaxation of the sumptuary laws during the duke's visit. The main source.

Studies

2. CONTARINI DEL ZAFFO, ALVISE CARLO, *Venuta e soggiorno a Venezia di Francesco Sforza duca di Milano dall'11 ottobre al 5 novembre 1530 e feste fatte in quella occasione.* N.p., Tip. della Società Marino Sanudo 1883, pp. 45 (Nozze Parravicino-Persia Benvenuti).

Publishes a number of reports soon to appear in Sanudo's *Diarii*, above, and also letters written by the duke and preserved in the Archivio di Stato of Milan. Provides a short introduction and numerous historical notes.

3. *Enciclopedia dello spettacolo*, under « Venezia », vol. IX, col. 1538.

A summary of the ceremonies and entertainments.

V

1549, May 28. Entry of Vittoria Farnese della Rovere, Duchess of Urbino.

The duchess, whose husband was « governatore delle armi » for the Venetian republic, was entertained in Chioggia on May 27. The next day she embarked for Venice. At Santo Spirito she was awaited by a delegation of Venetian gentlemen and, after changing boats, proceeded further, observing a naumachia along the way. At Sant'Antonio she was greeted by the doge and other officials and then proceeded in the Bucentaur, surrounded by small craft, to the Grand Canal, the facades of whose palaces had been decorated. Dancing on board. The Rialto bridge opened for her passage. The doge accompanied her to her lodgings.

Source

1. [PACE, POMPEO], *L'allegrezze e le dimostrazioni fatte nell'inclita citta di Venetia alla venuta dell'illustr. et eccel. Sig. Vittoria Farnesa Della Rovere duchessa d'Urbino.* N.p., n.d., probably Venice 1549, 8°, cc. 8. Bibliothèque de l'Arsenal, Paris: Fonds Rondel Ra⁵. 1439.

A detailed formal account addressed to the duchess herself. The source of all the above information.

Study

2. ROSSI PARISI, MATILDE, *Vittoria Farnese, duchessa d'Urbino.* Modena, Tip. G. Ferraguti 1927, pp. 57-58.

A good account of the duchess's reception, based on a ms. chronicle, with publication of an enthusiastic letter that the duchess wrote from Venice.

LIST OF WORKS THAT ARE RELEVANT TO MORE THAN ONE FESTIVAL AND RECEIVE ABBREVIATED CITATIONS IN THE TEXT

ADEMOLLO, ALESSANDRO, *Alessandro VI, Giulio II e Leone X nel carnevale di Roma. Documenti inediti (1490-1520).* Firenze, C. Ademollo 1886, pp. 93.

ALBERTINI, FRANCESCO, *Opusculum de mirabilibus novae urbis Romae,* herausgegeben von R. Schmarsow. Heilbronn, Verlag von Gebr. Henninger 1886, pp. xxiii-77. 1st. ed. 1510.

ALENDA Y MIRA, JENARO, *Relaciones de solemnidades y fiestas públicas de España, tomo primiero.* Madrid, Establecimiento Tipográfico « Successores de Rivadeneyra », 1903, pp. lxxxv-527.

ALVAREZ, VICENTE, *Relación del camino del Principe D. Felipe año de M.D.XLVIII. desde España á Italia, y por Alemania á Flandes y Bruselas, donde estaba su padre.* Place and publisher unknown, 1551. Biblioteca Nacional, Madrid. Not seen. Cited by ALENDA Y MIRA, *Relaciones de solemnidades y fiestas públicas de España,* p. 45 (item 132), and by Joseph Gillet (with a somewhat longer title) in a study related to the prince's visit to Milan, 1548-49, listed in our text.

ANONYMOUS, *Catalogue des livres rares et précieux composant la bibliothèque de M. E.-F.-D. Ruggieri. Sacres des rois et des empereurs, entrées triomphales, mariages, tournois, joûtes, carrousels, fêtes populaires et feux d'artifice.* Paris, Adolphe Labitte 1873.

ANONYMOUS, *Le Excellent et plus divin q'humain voyage entreprins et faict par plus que illustrissime prince Charles César toujours auguste [...] pour son couronnement, entree es Itales, embarquement, triumphe de Gennes [...] avec le recueil que lui a faict nostre sainct pere le pape a Bolongne la Grasse, et de lentree en icelle.* N.p., n.d., doubtless 1529 or 1530, 4º, cc. 4. Not seen. Cited in the anonymous *Catalogue des livres de M. Ruggieri,* above, pp. 181-182 (item 890), and by ALENDA Y MIRA, *Relaciones de solemnidades y fiestas públicas de España,* above, p. 25 (item 60).

ANONYMOUS, *Racconti di storia napoletana,* a cura di « D. ». « Archivio Storico per le Province Napoletane », vol. XXXIII, 1908, pp. 474-544 and 663-719; vol. XXXIV, 1909, pp. 78-117.

ANONYMOUS AND COLLECTIVE, *Recueil de pièces du temps, la plupart relatives aux expéditions de Charles VIII en Italie.* A collection of incunabulum pamphlets in the Bibliothèque Nationale, Paris, Rés. Lb^{28}. 1.

AUTON, JEAN D', *Chroniques de Jean d'Auton, publiées pour la première fois en entier d'après les manuscrits de la Bibliothèque du Roi*, avec une notice et des notes par Paul L. Jacob. Paris, Silvestre 1834-35, 4 tomes bound in 2 vols.

BARRILLON, JEAN, *Journal de Jean Barrillon, secrétaire du Chancelier Duprat 1515-1521*, publié pour la première fois pour la Société de l'Histoire de France par Pierre de Vaissière. Paris, Librairie Renouard 1897-1899, 2 vols.

BERNARDI, ANDREA (« NOVACULA »), *Cronache forlivesi di Andrea Bernardi Novacula dal 1476 al 1517, pubblicate ora per la prima volta di su l'autografo*, a cura di Giuseppe Mazzatinti. Bologna, R. Deputazione di Storia Patria 1895-97, 2 vols. bound in 3.

BONFADIO, JACOPO, *Annali delle cose di Genova dall'anno MDXXVIII sino all'anno MDL*, tradotti dal latino da Bartolomei Paschetti. Capolago, Tip. Elvetica 1836, pp. xlviii-240. Edition in Latin 1747; 1st. ed. of Paschetti's translation, 1597.

BUGATI, GASPARE, *Historia universale di M. Gaspare Bugati milanese, nella quale con ogni candidezza di verita si racconta brevemente, e con bell'ordine tutto quel ch'a successo dal principio del mondo fino all'anno M.D.L.XIX*. Venezia, Gabriel Giolito di Ferrarii 1570, 4º, pp. 1090. Biblioteca Nazionale Centrale, Florence: Palat. 19.4.4.10.

BURCHARD, JOHANN, *Diarium, sive rerum urbanarum commentarii, 1483-1506*, texte latin publié intégralement pour la première fois [...] avec introduction, notes [...] par Louis Thuasne. Paris, E. Leroux 1883-85, 3 tomes.

BURCHARD, JOHANN, *Johannis Burckardi liber notarum ab anno MCCCCLXXXIII usque ad annum MDVI*, a cura di Enrico Celani. In MURATORI, *Rerum italicarum scriptores*, tomo XXXIII, parte I, 2 vols.

BURCKHARDT, JACOB, *La civiltà del Rinascimento in Italia*, trad. italiana di D. Valbusa, 3ª edizione accresciuta per cura di Giuseppe Zippel. Firenze, Sansoni 1927, 2 vols. Original edition in German 1865.

BURIGOZZO, GIAN MARCO, *Cronica milanese di Gian Marco Burigozzo merzaro dal 1500 al 1544*, a cura di Cesare Cantù. « Archivio Storico Italiano », tomo III, 1842, pp. 421-552.

CAGNOLA, GIOVAN PIETRO, *Storia di Milano scritta da Giovan Pietro Cagnola, castellano della Rocca di Sartirana, dall'anno 1023 (omesso il primo libro) sino al 1497*, a cura di Cesare Cantù. « Archivio Storico Italiano », tomo III, 1842, pp. 2-215.

CALVETE DE ESTRELLA, JUAN, *El felicissimo viaje del muy alto y muy poderoso Príncipe Don Philippo, hijo d'el Emperador Don Carlos Quinto Maximo, desde Espana a sus tierras de la baxa Alemana*. Anversa, Martin Nucio 1552, 4º, cc. 355, numbered. Bibliothèque Nationale, Paris: Oc. 165. New Spanish edition in 2 vols., 1930; French translation in 5 vols., 1873-74.

CAMBI, GIOVANNI, *Istorie di Giovanni Cambi, cittadino fiorentino*, pubblicate e di annotazioni, e di antichi munimenti accresciute ed illustrate, da Fr. Ildefonso di San Luigi. Firenze,

Gaet. Cambiagi 1835-36 (« Delizie degli Eruditi Toscani », 29-33), 4 vols.

CANALE, MICHEL-GIUSEPPE, *Nuova istoria della repubblica di Genova, del suo commercio e della sua letteratura dalle origini all'anno 1797, narrata ed illustrata con note ed inediti documenti da Michel-Giuseppe Canale*. Firenze, Le Monnier 1858-64, 4 vols.

CANALE, MICHEL-GIUSEPPE, *Storia della repubblica di Genova dall'anno 1528 al 1550, ossia le congiure di Gian Luigi Fiesco e Giulio Cibo, colla luce di nuovi documenti*. Genova, Tip. del R. Istituto Sordo-Muti 1874, pp. 434.

CANCELLIERI, FRANCESCO, *Storia de' solenni possessi de' sommi pontefici detti anticamente processi o processioni dopo la loro coronazione dalla Basilica Vaticana alla Lateranense*. Roma, Luigi Lazzarini 1802, pp. xxxiv-544.

CARTWRIGHT, JULIA MARY (MRS. ADY), *Isabella d'Este, Marchioness of Mantua, 1474-1539: A Study of the Renaissance*. London, J. Murray; New York, E. P. Dutton 1903, 2 vols. Other editions as well.

CASONI, FILIPPO MARIA, *Annali della repubblica di Genova del secolo decimo sesto descritti da Filippo Casoni*. Genova, Antonio Casamara 1708, pp. lv-391.

CHARTROU, JOSÈPHE, *Les Entrées solennelles et triomphales à la Renaissance (1484-1551)*, thèse complémentaire pour le Doctorat ès Lettres. Paris, Presses Universitaires de France 1928, pp. 158.

CHASTEL, ANDRÉ, *Les Entrées de Charles-Quint en Italie*. In JACQUOT, ed., *Les Fêtes de la Renaissance II*, here listed, pp. 197-206.

CHERRIER, C. DE, *Histoire de Charles VIII roi de France, d'après des documents diplomatiques inédits ou nouvellement publiés*, 2e éd. Paris, Didier 1870, 2 vols.

CIMBER, M.-L., and DANJOU, F., eds., *Archives curieuses de l'histoire de France*. Paris, Beauvais 1834-35, tomes I and II. Cimber (whose real name was Lafaist) edited the first volume alone, while he and Danjou did the second together.

CLEMENTI, FILIPPO, *Il carnevale romano nelle cronache contemporanee, con illustrazioni riprodotte da stampe e quadri dell'epoca*. Roma, Tip. Tiberina di F. Setth 1899, pp. 587.

COMINES, PHILIPPE DE, *Mémoires*, édités par Joseph Calmette avec la collaboration du Chanoine G. Durville. Tome III: *1484-1498*. Paris, Champion 1925, pp. 442.

CREIGHTON, MANDELL, *A History of the Papacy during the Period of the Reformation*. London, Longmans and Green 1882-94, 5 vols.

CREIZENACH, WILHELM, *Geschichte des neueren Dramas*. Halle A. S., M. Niemeyer 1901-1909, 4 vols.

D'ANCONA, ALESSANDRO, *Origini del teatro italiano, libri tre*, 2ª ed. Torino, Loescher 1891, 2 vols. Anastatic reprint Roma, Bardi 1966.

DELABORDE, H.-FRANCOIS, *L'Expédition de Charles VIII en Italie: histoire diplomatique et militaire*. Paris, Firmin-Didot 1888, pp. viii-699.

DESJARDINS, ABEL, ed., *Négotiations diplomatiques de la France avec la Toscane*, documents recueillis par Giuseppe Canestrini et publiés par Abel Desjardins. Paris, Imprimerie Impériale 1859-72 (« Collection des documents inédits sur l'histoire de France,

1re serie, histoire politique »), 4 vols.

DESREY, PIERRE, *Relation du* [...] *voyage du Roy Charles VIII pour la conqueste du royaume de Naples*. Printed partly in GODEFROY, *Histoire de Charles VIII*, pp. 190-206; and in CIMBER, *Archives curieuses de l'histoire de France*, tome I, pp. 199-223, both of which are listed here.

EGGER, HERMANN, *Entwürfe Baldassare Peruzzis für den Einzüg Karls V. in Rom: eine Studie zur Frage über die Echtheit des Sienesischen Skizzenbuches*. « Jahrbuch der Kunsthistorischen Sammlungen des Allerhöchsten Kaiserhauses » (Wien, Prag, Leipzig), Band XXIII, Heft 1, 1902, pp. 1-44.

Enciclopedia dello spettacolo. Fondata da Silvio D'Amico. Sotto gli auspici della Fondazione Giorgio Cini. Roma, Le Maschere 1954-67, 9 vols.

EQUICOLA D'ALVETO, MARIO, *Dell'istoria di Mantova libri cinque scritta in commentari da Mario Equicola d'Alveto* [...], riformato secondo l'uso moderno di scrivere istorie per Benedetto Osanna Mantovano. Mantova, Francesco Osanna 1607, 4°, pp. 307.

FABBRI, MARIO, *et al.*, eds., *Il luogo teatrale a Firenze: Brunelleschi, Vasari, Buontalenti, Parigi*, catalogo a cura di Mario Fabbri, Elvira Garbero Zorzi, Anna Maria Petrioli Tofani. Catalogue of an exhibition held at the Museo Mediceo of the Palazzo Medici-Riccardi in Florence, May 31-October 31, 1975. Milano, Electa 1975 (« Spettacolo e musica nella Firenze medicea, documenti e restituzioni », 1), pp. 169. Ludovico Zorzi's very useful introduction to

this volume is cited rather in its revised version published in his *Il teatro e la città*, here listed.

FABBRI, PAOLO, *Gusto scenico a Mantova nel tardo Rinascimento*. Padova, Liviana 1973, pp. 65.

FABRONI, ANGELO, *Leonis X Pontificis Maximi vita auctore Angelo Fabronio academiae pisanae curatore*. Pisa, Alexander Landius 1797, pp. 330.

FACCIOLI, EMILIO, ed., *Mantova: le lettere*, vol. II. Mantova, Istituto Carlo d'Arco per la Storia di Mantova 1962, pp. xii-668.

FIORANI, L., *Riti ceremonie feste e vita di popolo nella Roma dei papi*. Bologna, Cappelli 1970 (« Roma cristiana », 12), pp. 343.

FLORANGE (or FLEURANGES), ROBERT DE LA MARCK, SEIGNEUR DE, *Mémoires du Maréchal de Florange, dit le petit aventureux*, publiés pour la Société de l'Histoire de France par Robert Goubaix et P.-André Lemoisne. Paris, Renouard 1913-1924, 2 tomes.

FOGLIETTA, UBERTO, *Dell'istorie di Genova di Mons. Uberto Foglietta patrizio genovese, libri XII*, tradotte per M. Francesco Serdonati. Genova, Heredi di Girolamo Bartoli 1597, folio, pp. lv-644. Anastatic reprint Bologna, Forni 1969. The original Latin edition had appeared in 1585.

FONTANA, BARTOLOMMEO, *Renata di Francia duchessa di Ferrara, sui documenti dell'Archivio Estense, del Mediceo, del Gonzaga e dell'Archivio Secreto Vaticano*. Roma, Forzani 1889-99, 3 vols.

FORCELLA, VINCENZO, *Tornei e giostre, ingressi trionfali in Roma sotto Paolo III (1534-1549)*. Roma, Tip. Artigianelli 1885, pp. 116. On a separate page there appears also the title *Feste in Roma nel pontificato di Paolo III, 1534-1549*. Anastatic reprint, Bologna, Forni 1971.

FRIZZI, ANTONIO, *Memorie per la storia di Ferrara*, raccolte da Antonio Frizzi, con giunte e note del Conte Avv. Camillo Laderchi, 2ª ed. Ferrara, Abram Servadio 1847-50, 5 vols.

FROMMEL, CHRISTOPH LUITPOLD, *Baldassare Peruzzi als Maler und Zeichner*, Beiheft zum « Römischer Jahrbuch fur Kunstgeschichte », Band II, 1967-68. Wien-München, Verlag Anton Schroll 1967-68, pp. 183.

GACHARD, LOUIS PROSPER, ed., *Collection des voyages des souverains des Pays-Bas*. Bruxelles, F. Hayez, Imprimeur de la Commission Royale d'Histoire 1874-82 (« Chroniqueurs belges »), 4 tomes.

GHISI, FEDERICO, *Feste musicali della Firenze medicea (1480-1589)*. Firenze, Vallecchi 1939, pp. xlviii-94.

GIACOMO, IL NOTAR, *Cronaca di Napoli di Notar Giacomo*, pubblicata per cura di Paolo Garzilli. Napoli, Stamperia Reale 1945, pp. vii-360.

GIONTA, STEFANO, ed., *Il Fioretto delle cronache di Mantova, raccolto da Stefano Gionta, notabilmente accresciuto e continuato sino all'anno MDCCCLIV per cura di Antonio Mainardi*. Mantova, Negretti 1844, pp. 383. Anastatic reprint Mantova, Istituto Carlo d'Arco per la Storia di Mantova 1972.

GIUSTINIANI, AGOSTINO, *Annali della repubblica di Genova scritti da Monsignore Agostino Giustiniani corretti ed illustrati*. Genova, Tip. Giovanni Ferrando 1834-35, 2 vols.

GNOLI, DOMENICO, *La Roma di Leone X, quadri e studi originali annotati e pubblicati a cura di Aldo Gnoli*. Milano, Hoepli 1938, pp. xix-388.

GODEFROY, THEODORE and DENYS, *Le Cérémonial françois, tome premier, contenant les cérémonies observées en France aux sacres et couronnements de roys, et reynes, et de quelques anciens ducs de Normandie, d'Aquitaine, et de Bretagne: comme aussi à leurs entrées solennelles: et à celles d'aucuns dauphins, gouverneurs de provinces, et autres seigneurs, dans diverses villes du royaume*, recueilly par Théodore Godefroy, conseiller du roy en ses conseils et mis en lumière par Denys Godefroy, advocat au parlement et historiographe du roy. Paris, Sébastien et Gabriel Cramoisy 1649, folio. The earlier edition of this work, entitled *Le Cérémonial de France*, does not contain the material about the entries of French kings in Italy.

GODEFROY, THEODORE, ed., *Histoire de Charles VIII roy de France par Guillaume de Jaligny, André de la Vigne et autres historiens de ce temps-là* [...]. Paris, Sébastien Mabre Cramoisy, Imprimerie Royale 1684, folio, pp. 759.

[GONZAGA, LUIGI], *Cronaca del soggiorno di Carlo V in Italia (dal 26 luglio al 25 aprile 1530), documento di storia italiana estratto da un codice della Regia Biblioteca Universitaria di Pavia*, [a cura di Giacinto Romano]. Milano, Hoepli 1892, pp. 286. Though the ms. of this work bore no indication of the author's identity, the editor has shown that it was almost certainly written by Luigi Gonzaga.

GORI, PIETRO, *Le feste fiorentine attraverso i secoli: le feste di San Giovanni*.

Firenze, Bemporad 1926, pp. viii-338.

GORI, PIETRO, *Firenze magnifica: le feste fiorentine attraverso i secoli*. Firenze, Bemporad 1930, pp. 314.

GRASSI, PARIDE DE', *Il diario di Leone X di Paride de' Grassi*, a cura di Mons. Pio Delicati e Mariano Armellini. Roma, Tip. della Pace 1884, pp. xii-128.

GRASSI, PARIDE DE', *Le sue spedizioni militari di Giulio II, tratte dal diario di Paride Grassi* [...], con note e documenti di Luigi Frati. Bologna, Regia Tip. 1886 («Documenti e studi pubblicati per cura della R. Deputazione di Storia Patria per le Province di Romagna», 1), pp. 363.

[GRAVIER, GIOVANNI], ed., *Raccolta di tutti i più rinomati scrittori dell'istoria generale del regno di Napoli principiando dal tempo che queste provincie hanno preso forma di regno*. Tomi VI and VIII. Napoli, Giovanni Gravier 1769-70. Gravier is both the editor and the publisher. The various works published in these volumes usually have separate pagination.

GREGOROVIUS, FERDINAND, *Lucrezia Borgia secondo documenti e carteggi del tempo*, a cura di Angelo Romano, traduzione di Luigi Quattrocchi, introduzione di Mario Martinelli. Roma, Salerno Editrice 1978 («Omicron», 4), pp. 391. Original edition in German, 1874; other editions in Italian, as well as in English and French.

GUASTI, CESARE, *Le feste di San Giovanni Battista in Firenze descritte in prosa e in rima da contemporanei*. Firenze, Ermanno Loescher-Fratelli Bocca 1884, pp. vii-108.

GUICCIARDINI, FRANCESCO, *Storia d'Ita-lia*, a cura di Costantino Panigada. Bari, Laterza 1929 («Scrittori d'Italia», 120-124), 5 vols.

HARTT, FREDERICK, *Giulio Romano*. New Haven, Connecticut, Yale University Press 1961, 2 vols.

JACQUOT, JEAN, ed., *Les Fêtes de la Renaissance II: fêtes et cérémonies au temps de Charles-Quint*. IIe Congrès de l'Association Internationale des Historiens de la Renaissance (2e section), Bruxelles, Anvers, Gand, Liège, 2-7 septembre, 1957. Paris, Centre National de la Recherche Scientifique 1960, pp. 518 and 47 plates.

JACQUOT, JEAN, ed., *Les Fêtes de la Renaissance III*. 15e Colloque International d'Etudes Humanistes, Tours, 10-22 Juillet, 1972. Paris, Centre National de la Recherche Scientifique 1975, pp. 661.

JACQUOT, JEAN, *Panorama des fêtes et cérémonies du règne* [*de Charles-Quint*], in JACQUOT, *Les Fêtes de la Renaissance II*, here listed, pp. 413-491.

LANCIANI, RODOLFO, *Storia degli scavi di Roma e notizie intorno le collezioni romane di antichità*. Roma, Ermanno Loescher 1902-12, 4 vols.

LANDUCCI, LUCA, *Diario fiorentino dal 1450 al 1516, continuato da un anonimo fino al 1542*, pubblicato sui codici della Communale di Siena e della Marucelliana con annotazioni da Iodoco del Badia. Firenze, Sansoni 1883, pp. xv-377.

LA PILORGERIE, JULES DE, *Campagne et bulletins de la Grande Armée d'Italie commandée par Charles VIII 1494-*

1495, *d'après des documents rares ou inédits* [...]. Nantes, V. Forest et E. Grimaud; Paris, Didier 1866, pp. xxxviii-475.

LAPINI, AGOSTINO, *Diario fiorentino di Agostino Lapini dal 252 al 1596*, ora pubblicato da Giuseppe Odoardo Corazzini. Firenze, Sansoni 1900, pp. xxvii-384.

LA VIGNE, ANDRE DE, *Histoire du voyage de Naples du Roy Charles VIII*, in GODEFROY, *Histoire de Charles VIII*, here listed, pp. 114-189. This account, almost identical to La Vigne's relation of Charles' expedition in the *Vergier d'honneur*, here listed, is cited in conjunction with it in the bibliography.

[LA VIGNE, ANDRE DE], *La Tres Curieuse et Chevaleresque Hystoire de la Conqueste de Naples par Charles VIII, comment le tres chrestien et tres victorieux Roy Charles huictiesme de ce nom, a banniere deployee, passa et repassa de journee en journee de Lyon jusques a Naples et de Naples jusques a Lyon*, publiée par P.-M. Gonon. Lyon, Imprimerie de Dumoulin, Ronet et Sihuet 1842, pp. 196. This account, though published as anonymous, is so similar to those in LA VIGNE's *Histoire du voyage de Naples* and *Vergier d'honneur* that it clearly derives from them. In the bibliography it is cited in conjunction with the *Vergier*.

LA VIGNE, ANDRE DE, and SAINT GELAIS, OCTOVIEN DE, *Le Vergier d'honneur nouvellement imprime a Paris. Auquel est comprins comment le Roy Charles huitiesme de ce nom a banjere deployee passa et repassa de iournee depuis Lyon iusques a Naples, et de Naples jusques a Lyon. Ensemble ply sieurs aultres choses faictes et composees par reverend pere en Dieu Monsieur Octavien de Saint Gelais evesque dangoulesme et par maistres Andry de la Vigne secretaire de la royne et de monsieur le duc de Savoye, avec aultres.* N.p., n.d., probably Paris, ca. 1500, folio, 6 leaves per signature, sigs. a-t and A-P. Bibliothèque Nationale, Paris: Rés. Lb28.5α. There are several other editions of this work, most of them in the very early sixteenth century, but none of them I have seen contain the very interesting woodcuts of the edition cited here. The second half of La Vigne's account of Charles VIII's Italian expedition in the *Vergier d'honneur* is reprinted in CIMBER, *Archives curieuses de l'histoire de France*, here listed, tome I, pp. 314-435. I have found no modern edition of the first half of the account.

LUZIO, A., and RENIER, R., *Mantova e Urbino: Isabella d'Este ed Elisabetta Gonzaga nelle relazioni famigliari e nelle vicende politiche*. Torino-Roma, L. Roux 1893, pp. xv-333.

MANGO, ACHILLE, *La commedia in lingua nel Cinquecento, bibliografia critica*. Firenze, Lerici 1966, pp. 290.

MAROT DE CAEN, JEAN, *Ian Marot de Caen sur les deux heureux voyages de Genes et Venise, victorieusement mys a fin par le treschrestien Roy Loys douxiesme de ce nom* [...]. Lyon, Francoys Iuste 1537, 16°, cc. 134, numbered. Bibliothèque Nationale, Paris: Rés. Yᵉ. 1440. Earlier edition, 1532.

MASI, BARTOLOMEO, *Ricordanze di Bartolomeo Masi calderaio fiorentino dal 1478 al 1526*, per la prima volta pubblicate da Giuseppe Odoardo Corazzini. Firenze, Sansoni 1906, pp. xxii-311.

MAZZOLDI, LEONARDO, ed., *Mantova: la storia*, vol. II: *da Ludovico secondo marchese a Francesco secondo duca*. Mantova, Istituto Carlo d'Arco per la Storia di Mantova 1961, pp. xv-541.

MITCHELL, BONNER, *Les Intermèdes au service de l'Etat*, in JACQUOT, *Les Fêtes de la Renaissance III*, here listed, pp. 117-131.

MOLMENTI, POMPEO GHERARDO, *La storia di Venezia nella vita privata dalle origini alla caduta della repubblica*, 4ª edizione interamente rifatta. Bergamo, Istituto Italiano d'Arti Grafiche 1905-1908, 3 vols.

MONTOICHE, GUILLAUME DE, *Voyage et expédition de Charles-Quint aux pays de Tunis*, in GACHARD, *Collection des voyages des souverains des Pays-Bas*, here listed, vol. III, pp. 317-388.

MURATORI, LUDOVICO ANTONIO, *Delle antichità estensi continuazione o sia parte seconda*. Modena, Stamperia Ducale 1740, pp. 736.

MURATORI, LUDOVICO ANTONIO, ed., *Rerum italicarum scriptores, ordinata da L. A. Muratori*, nuova edizione riveduta amplificata e corretta con la direzione di Giosuè Carducci e Vittorio Fiorini. Città di Castello, S. Lapi; for some volumes, Bologna, Zanichelli 1900-.

MUZZI, SALVATORE, *Annali della citta di Bologna dalla sua origine al 1796 compilate da Salvatore Muzzi*. Bologna, Tipi di S. Tommaso d'Aquino 1840-46, 8 vols.

NARDI, JACOPO, *Istorie di Firenze di Jacopo Nardi*, a cura di Agenore Gelli. Firenze, Le Monnier 1858, 2 vols.

NICOLINI, FAUSTO, *Sul viaggio di Filippo d'Asburgo in Italia (1547-48)*. « Banco di Napoli: Bollettino dell'Archivio Storico », fasc. 9-12, puntata prima, 1955-56, pp. 204-266. The date given in the title should be 1548-49.

PASCHINI, PIO, *Roma nel Rinascimento*, vol. XII of the *Storia di Roma* published by the Istituto di Studi Romani. Bologna, Cappelli 1940, pp. xxvi-526.

PASSERO, GIULIANO, *Giuliano Passero, cittadino napoletano, o sia prima pubblicazione in istampa, che delle storie in forma di giornale, le quali sotto il nome di questo autore finora erano andate manoscritte, ora si fa da Vincenzo Maria Altobelli*. Napoli, V. Orsino 1785, pp. 148 (introd.) and 351.

PASTOR, LUDWIG, *Storia dei papi dalla fine del Medio Evo, compilata col sussidio dell'Archivio Segreto pontificio e di molti altri archivi*, nuova versione italiana sulla IVª edizione originale del Sac. Angelo Mercati, poi versione italiana di Pio Cenci. Roma, Desclee e C. Editore 1910-34, 16 vols. of which some are divided into separately published parts. Original edition in German 1901-33. English and French translations.

PAULLO, AMBROGIO DA, *Cronaca milanese dall'anno 1476 al 1515 di Maestro Ambrogio da Paullo*, edita da Antonio Ceruti. « Miscellanea di Storia Italiana », tomo XIII, 1871, pp. 93-378.

PECCHIAI, PIO, *Roma nel Cinquecento*, vol. XIII of the *Storia di Roma* published by the Istituto di Studi

Romani. Bologna, Cappelli 1948, pp. xx-593.

PECCI, GIOVAN ANTONIO, Memorie storico-critiche della città di Siena [...] raccolte dal Signor Cavaliere Giovan Antonio Pecci. Siena, Agostino Bindi 1755-60, 4 vols.

[PELLICCIA, A. A.], ed., Raccolta di varie croniche diarj, ed altri opuscoli così italiani come latini appartenenti alla storia del regno di Napoli di Pietro Giannone. Napoli, Bernardo Perger 1780, 5 tomi.

PERRENS, FRANÇOIS-TOMMY, Histoire de Florence depuis la domination des Médicis jusqu'à la chute de la république (1434-1531). Paris, Quantin 1888-1890, 3 tomes.

PIRROTTA, NINO, Li due Orfei : dal Poliziano a Monteverdi, con un saggio critico sulla scenografia di Elena Povoledo, 2ª ed. Torino, Einaudi 1975, pp. xv-472.

PONTIERI, ERNESTO, et al., Storia di Napoli. Napoli, Società Editrice Storia di Napoli 1967-74, 10 vols.

POSSEVINO, ANTONIO, Antonii Possevini iunioris philosophi et medici mantuani Gonzaga; Calci operis addita genealogia totius familiae. Mantua, apud Osannas Fratres ducales typographos 1628, folio, pp. 858.

POVOLEDO, ELENA, Origini e aspetti della scenografia in Italia, dalla fine del Quattrocento agli intermezzi fiorentini del 1589, in PIRROTTA, Li due Orfei, here listed, pp. 337-460.

PRATO, GIOVANNI ANDREA, Storia di Milano scritta da Giovanni Andrea Prato, patrizio milanese, in continuazione ed emenda del Corio dall'anno 1499 sino al 1519, a cura di Cesare Cantù. « Archivio Storico Italiano », tomo III, 1842, pp. 219-418.

PRIULI, GIROLAMO, I diarii di Girolamo Priuli (AA. 1494-1512), a cura di Arturo Segre e Roberto Cessi, in MURATORI, Rerum italicarum scriptores, here listed, tomo XXIV, parte III, 4 vols. The volumes published go only to 1509.

PROVEDI, ABBATE AGOSTINO, Relazione delle pubbliche feste date in Siena negli ultimi cinque secoli [...]. Siena, Luigi e Benedetto Bindi 1791, pp. 160.

RABELAIS, FRANÇOIS, Oeuvres complètes, ed. Pierre Jourda. Paris, Garnier 1963, 2 vols.

RINALDI, ODORICO, Annales ecclesiastici ab anno MCXCVIII ubi desinit Cardinalis Baronius, auctore Odorico Raynaldo [...], tomi XI-XIV. Lucae, Typis Leonardi Venturini 1754-55.

RODOCANACHI, EMMANUEL, Histoire de Rome : le pontificat de Jules II, 1503-1513. Paris, Hachette 1928, pp. 196.

RODOCANACHI, EMMANUEL, Histoire de Rome : le pontificat de Léon X, 1513-1521. Paris, Hachette 1932, pp. 308.

RODOCANACHI, EMMANUEL, Histoire de Rome : les pontificats d'Adrien VI et de Clément VII. Paris, Hachette 1933, pp. 292.

RODOCANACHI, EMMANUEL, Histoire de Rome : une cour princière au Vatican pendant la Renaissance, Sixte IV, Innocent VIII, Alexandre VI Borgia, 1471-1503. Paris, Hachette 1925, pp. 315.

RODOCANACHI, EMMANUEL, Une protectrice de la Réforme en Italie et en France, Renée de France, Duchesse de Ferrare. Paris, Ollendorff 1896, pp. 573.

ROSCOE, WILLIAM, Vita e pontificato di Leone X di Guglielmo Roscoe [...], tradotta e corredata di annotazioni e di alcuni documenti inediti dal Conte Cav. Luigi Bossi. Milano, Tip. Sonzogno e Come 1816-17, 12 vols.

[SALA, ANDREA], *Ordini, pompe, apparati et ceremonie delle solenne intrate di Carlo. V. Imp. sempre Aug. nella citta di Roma, Siena et Fiorenza.* N.p., n.d., but 1536, 4º, sigs. A-D. Biblioteca Riccardiana, Florence: Moren. B 5 64. British Museum, London: 1318, c. 7 (1).

[SALA, ANDREA], *La triomphale entrata di Carlo. V. Imperatore Augusto in la inclita citta di Napoli, e di Messina, con il significato delli archi triumphali, e delle figure antiche in prosa e versi latini.* N.p., n.d., but 1536, 4º, sigs. A-C. Biblioteca Riccardiana, Florence: Moren. B 5 64. British Museum, London: 1318 c 7.

SANESI, IRENEO, *Storia dei generi letterari italiani: la commedia,* 2ª ed. Milano, Vallardi 1954, 2 vols.

SANTA CRUZ, ALONSO DE, *Crónica del Emperador Carlos V compuesta por Alonso de Santa Cruz su cosmógrafo major [...], publicada [...] por D. Ricardo Beltrán y Rózpide y Don Antonio Blasquez y Delgado-Aguilera.* Madrid, Imprenta del Patronato de Huérfanos 1920-25, 5 vols.

SANUDO, MARINO, *I diarii di Marino Sanuto (MCCCCXCVI-MDXXXIII),* a cura di Rinaldo Fulin *et al.* per la Deputazione Veneta di Storia Patria. Venezia, F. Visentini 1879-1913, 58 vols. Anastatic reprint Bologna, Forni 1969-70.

SANUDO, MARINO, *La spedizione di Carlo VIII in Italia, raccontata da Marino Sanudo* e pubblicata a cura di Rinaldo Fulin. Venezia, F. Visentini 1883, pp. 677.

SARDI, GASPARO, *Libro delle historie ferraresi de Sig. Gasparo Sardi, con una nuova aggiunta del medesimo autore. Aggiuntivi di più quattro libri del Sig. Dottore Faustini sino alla devoluzione del ducato di Ferrara alla Santa Sede, con le tavole di tutti gli due libri.* Ferrara, Giuseppe Gironi 1646, 4º, pp. 230 and 182 (separate pagination for the parts written by Sardi and Faustini).

SENAREGA, BARTOLOMMEO, *Bartholomaei Senaregae de rebus genuensibus commentaria ab anno MCDLXXXVIII usque ad annum MDXIV,* a cura di Emilio Pandiani. In MURATORI, *Rerum italicarum scriptores,* here listed, tomo XXIV, parte VIII, pp. xliv-258.

STRONG, ANTHONY, *Splendour at Court: Renaissance Spectacle and Illusion.* London, Weidenfeld and Nicolson 1973, pp. 287.

SUMMONTE, GIOVAN ANTONIO, *Dell'historia della città e regno di Napoli.* Napoli, Antonio Bulifon 1640-75, 4 tomi. Later ed., 1748-50.

TEDALLINI, SEBASTIANO DI BRANCA, *Diario romano dal 3 maggio 1485 al 6 giugno 1524 [...],* a cura di Paolo Piccolomini. In MURATORI, *Rerum italicarum scriptores,* here listed, tomo XXIII, parte III, pp. 230-446.

TRECCANI DEGLI ALFIERI, CONTE GIOVANNI, ed., *Storia di Milano.* Milano, Fondazione Treccani degli Alfieri per la Storia di Milano 1953-66, 16 vols. and index.

TRUFFI, RICCARDO, *Giostre e cantori di giostre; studi e ricerche di storia e di letteratura.* Rocca San Casciano, Cappelli 1911, pp. 228.

ULLOA, ALFONSO, *Vita e fatti dell'invitissimo Imperatore Carlo Quinto, et historie universali del mondo, de' suoi tempi* [...]. Venezia, Alessandro Vecchi 1606, 4º, cc. 255, numbered. Several earlier editions.

VANDENESSE, JEAN DE, *Journal des voyages de Charles-Quint de 1514 à 1551*, in GACHARD, *Collection des voyages des souverains des Pays-Bas*, here listed, vol. II, pp. 53-490.

VARCHI, BENEDETTO, *Storia fiorentina di Benedetto Varchi*, a cura di Lelio Arbib. Firenze, Società Editrice delle Storie del Nardi e del Varchi 1838-41, 3 vols.

VASARI, GIORGIO, *Le opere di Giorgio Vasari*, con nuove annotazioni e commenti di Gaetano Milanesi. Firenze, Sansoni 1878-85, 9 vols. Includes both the *Vite* and minor historical writings of Vasari.

VIZANI, POMPEO, *Di Pompeo Vizani gentil'huomo bolognese dieca libri delle historie della sua patria* [...]. Bologna, Giovanni Rossi 1602-08, 8º, 2 *parti* or volumes.

ZAMBOTTI, BERNARDINO, *Diario ferrarese dall'anno 1476 al 1504*, a cura di Giuseppe Pardi, in MURATORI, *Rerum italicarum scriptores*, here listed, tomo XXIV, parte VII, pp. xxxvi-500.

ZORZI, LUDOVICO, *Il teatro e la città: saggi sulla scena italiana*. Torino, Einaudi 1977, pp. xx-363.

ADDENDA

Pp. 17-19: Bologna, II, 1515.

Additional Commentary for a Study

FROMMEL, *Baldassare Peruzzi als Maler und Zeichner*, pp. 13 and 76 and plate xcii c. (Listed p. 18 above).

On re-reading, it becomes clear that the author thinks the sketch may have been a project of Peruzzi for an *apparato* to honor Francis I at Bologna. There is no evidence that the project was executed.

Additional Source

GIOVIO, PAOLO, *Pauli Iovii novocomensis episcopi nucerini, de vita Leonis Decimi Pont. Max. libri IIII* [...]. Florentiae, Ex Officina Laurentii Torrentini 1547, 4°, pp. 83-84. Biblioteca Nazionale, Florence: Rinasc. Medici 114.

Quite a spare account of the pope's entry and stay in Bologna by a member of his entourage.

P. 27: Cremona, II, 1549.

Additional Commentary for a Source

SANTA CRUZ, *Crónica del Emperador Carlos V*, vol. V, p. 257.

Now seen. A short account with some information on the emperor's reception, but nothing on the *apparati*.

Pp. 46–48: Florence, V, 1536.

Additional Source

SCHEURL, CHRISTOPH, *Mit was Ehrerpietung des heiligen Reichs Statt Senis und der Hertzog von Florenz jren Herrn den Römischen Keiser den 24. und 28. Aprilis. 1536. empfangen haben. Summarie aus Welschem verteutscht*, interprete C. Scheurl. Nuremberg, J. Petri 1536, 4°. British Museum, London: 1315. b. 46.

Not seen. The account is apparently second hand and may be simply a translation of Sala (listed above, p. 47), but the author may have used other sources as well.

Pp. 117–119: Rome, V, 1513.

Additional Source

GIOVIO, *De vita Leonis decimi* (full citation above in these Addenda), pp. 69 and 71.

A short account by a possible witness, with the texts of two inscriptions.

Additional Study

FABRONI, *Leonis X vita* (full citation above, p. 152), pp. 64–65 and 270–274.

An account of the *possesso* with few details about the *apparati* and (pp. 270–274) a long quotation from the ms. history of Siena of Sigismondo Tizio, which contains more details and the texts of a number of inscriptions.

Pp. 119–124: Rome, VI, 1513.

Additional Study

FABRONI, *Leonis X vita* (full citation above, p. 152), pp. 83–84 and 276.

A short general narration of the festivities and a quotation from Sereno's account (listed p. 122).

Pp. 125-129: Rome, VII, 1536.

Additional Source

SCHEURL, CHRISTOPH, *Einrit Keyser Carlen in die alten keyserlichen Haubstatt Rom den 5. Aprilis. Aus allerlei welschen und teutschen Missiven* [...]. Nuremberg, F. Petrius 1536, 4°. British Museum, London: 1315. b. 39.

Not seen. The account is apparently second hand, but it is possible that the author took from German dispatches some information not recorded elsewhere.

Pp. 136-138: Siena, II, 1536.

Additional Source

SCHEURL, CHRISTOPH, *Mit was Ehrerpietung* [...], full citation above in these Addenda.

Not seen. The account is apparently second hand and may be simply a translation of Sala (listed above, p. 137), but the author may have used other sources as well.

P. 149: An Additional Work with Abbreviated Citations in the Text.

AMADEI, FEDERICO, *Cronaca universale della città di Mantova*, a cura di Giuseppe Amadei, Ercolano Marani, e Giovanni Praticò. Mantova, C.I.T.M. 1957, 3 vols.

INDEXES

EXPLANATION OF THE INDEXES

In consideration of the different uses to which this bibliography may be put, it has seemed wise to make several different indexes. That of the principal elements of *feste* will enable specialists to find quickly at least a few of the things in which they are most interested. That of artists, literary authors, and composers should be useful for art historians, literary and theatrical scholars, and musicologists. In this list I have tried to include all the names mentioned in the printed sources and studies, though one might well, of course, find others in archival or other unpublished material. The index of titles of literary works and first lines of musical compositions is complete (with the addition of the first lines of the compositions for the Florentine celebrations of 1539, omitted in the text), except that I have not indexed the untitled verses recited in certain *feste*. The list of participants and of personages and personifications in the *apparati* and dramatic presentations is, on the other hand, quite incomplete because of the limited scope of the summaries in the main text. The most important participants are, I trust, included, but there were many others, mentioned, for example, in this lists of the processions found in sources. Orators and organizers of festivals are included here, but artists, authors, and composers, indexed separately, are not, unless they have been mentioned as having some personal role in the proceedings. I had hesitated to index any of the figures from the *apparati* and dramatic presentations, because of the cursory nature of the summaries, but decided that even a partial list might present some interest. Scholars are, however, advised again, as in the preface, that complete lists and analyses in this category can be found only in the sources themselves.

For all the indexes except the last, the reference is to the treatment of a festival as a whole, with mention of the city, the number given to the festival in the text, and inclusive page numbers. It seemed impractical, for example, to mention a triumphal entering sovereign, or an artist who worked on the *apparati*, only for the pages on which his name occurred, while sources and studies throughout the treatment might be relevant. References in the index of authors of sources and studies and scholarly editors, a different case, are, however, to specific pages.

Arches, triumphal: Bologna, I (15-17), II (17-19), III (19-25); Cremona, I (26-27), II (27); Ferrara, III (32-34); Florence, I (35-37), III (39-43), V (46-48); VI (48-50), VII (50-54), VIII (55); Genoa, III (60-61), IV (61-63); Lucca, II (65-66); Mantua, I (68-70), III (72-74), IV (74-75); Messina, I (76-78); Milan, I (79-80), III (81-83), IV (83-85), V (85-86), VII (88-89), VIII (89-91), IX (91-94); Naples, III (99-100), IV (101-104); Pavia, I (105-106), III (107); Pisa, I, (108-110); Rome, III (114-115), V (117-119), VII (125-129), VIII (129-130); Siena, I (135-136), II (136-148); and Trent, I (138-140).
Automi, see *Machines*.

Chariots: Florence, I (35-37), II (38-39), V (46-48), VIII (55); Messina, I (76-78); Milan, I (79-80), III (81-83), IV (83-85); Naples, II (96-99), IV (101-104); Rome, II (113-114), III (114-115), IV (116); and Venice, I (143-144).
Comedies: Bologna, III (19-25); Ferrara, I (28-30), II (31-32), III (32-34); Florence, IV (43-46), VI (48-50), VII (50-54); Mantua, I (68-70), II (70-72), IV (74-75); Milan, IX (91-94); Naples, IV (101-104); Rome, II (113-114), VI (119-124), X (131-132); Siena, II (136-138); Venice, IV (147).

Drawings, woodcuts, commemorative paintings and other surviving graphic material: Bologna, II (17-19), III (19-25); Florence, I (35-37), II (38-39), III (39-43), VII (50-54); Mantua, I (68-70), II (70-72); Messina, I (76-78); Milan, VIII (89-91), IX (91-94); Pisa, I (108-110); Rome, I (111-112), V (117-119), VI (119-124), VII (125-129); Siena, I (135-136).

Games (jousts, naumachias, sciomachias, regattas etc.): Ferrara, III (32-34); Florence, VIII (55); Mantua, IV (74-75); Milan, III (81-83), VI (86-88), VIII (89-91), IX (91-94); Naples, IV (101-104); Rome, II (113-114), IX (130-131); Trent, I (138-140); Venice, II (144-146), IV (147), V (148).

Inscriptions on apparati (recorded): Bologna, I (15-17), II, (17-19), III (19-25); Cremona, I (26-27), II (27); Ferrara, III (32-34); Florence, I (35-37), V (46-48), VII (50-54); Genoa, III (60-61), IV (61-63); Lucca, I (64-65), II (65-66), III (66-67); Mantua, III (72-74); Messina, I (76-78); Milan, III (81-83), IV (83-85), V (85-86), VI (86-88), VII (88-89), VIII (89-91), IX (91-94); Naples, IV (101-104); Pavia, II (106), III (107); Rome, III (114-115), V (117-119), VI (119-124), VII (125-129), VIII (129-130), X (131-132); Savona, I (133-134); Siena, I (135-136), II (136-138); Trent, I (138-140); Turin, I (141-142); Venice, I (143-144).
Intermedii of comedies, nummeries and other short dramatic presentations for palace and theatre entertainments: Ferrara, I (28-30); Florence VI (48-50), VII (50-54); Milan, IX (91-94); Rome, II (113-114), VI (119-124); Venice, II (144-146), IV (147).

« *Machines* », or « *automi* »: Genoa, III (60-61), IV (61-63); Messina, I (76-78); Milan, VI (86-88), Naples, I (95-96), II (96-99), IV (101-104); Trent, I (138-140).

Mummeries, see *Intermedii*.

Mystères, tableaux vivants, and other dramatic presentations in the streets and piazzas: Ferrara, I (28-30); Florence, III (39-43); Genoa, II (58-60); Lucca, I (64-65); Milan, III (81-83), IV (83-85), V (85-86); Naples, III (99-100); Pavia, I (105-106); Pisa, I (108-110), Rome, III (114-115), V (117-119), IX (130-131); Siena, I (135-136).

Music, identified and preserved: Florence, VII (50-54); *apparently not preserved but with the names of the composers or performers recorded*: Ferrara, III (32-34); Genoa, IV (61-63); Venice, II (144-146). Music is mentioned briefly in the accounts of virtually all the other festivals.

Naumachias, see *Games*.

Regattas, see *Games*.

Sciomachias, see *Games*.

Tableaux vivants, see *Mystères*.

Verses, recited (recorded): Florence, II (38-39), VII (50-54); Milan, III (81-83), V (85-86), IX (91-94); Rome, VI (119-124); Siena, I (135-136); Trent, I (138-140); Venice, I (143-144), II (144-146). *Apparently not recorded*: Ferrara, I (28-30), Florence, III (39-43); Genoa, III (60-61); Naples, III (99-100); Pavia, I (105-106); Rome, II (113-114), V (117-119).

Woodcuts, see *Drawings*.

ARTISTS, AUTHORS OF PLAYS AND VERSES, COMPOSERS AND MUSICIANS

Alamanni, Antonio (author): Florence, II (38-39).

Alessandrino, Vittorio, see Vittorio Alessandrino.

Andrea del Sarto (artist): Florence, II (38-39), III (39-43).

Andrea di Salvi Barili (artist): Florence, I (35-37).

Antonio (di Donnino) di Domenico (artist): Florence, VII (50-54).

Antonio di Jacopo (artist): Florence, I (35-37).

Antonio di Marco di Giano, see Carota, il.

Ariosto, Ludovico (author): Ferrara, II (31-32).

Armonio (author): Venice, II (144-146).

Aspertini, Amico (artist): Bologna, III (19-25).

Baccio d'Agnolo (Baglioni) (artist): Florence, V (46-48).

Baccio da Montelupo (artist): Florence, III (39-43).

Bachiacca, il, see Ubertini, Francesco.

Baglioni, Baccio d'Agnolo, see Baccio d'Agnolo.

Baglioni, Giuliano (artist): Florence, V (46-48).

Bagnacavallo, il, see Aspertini, Amico.

Baia, il, see Jacopo di Bonaccorso.

Bandinelli, Baccio (artist): Florence, II (38-39), III (39-43).

Bandinelli, Bartolommeo, see Bandinelli, Baccio.

Barili, Andrea di Salvi, see Andrea di Salvi Barili.

Battista Franco (artist): Florence, V (46-48), VI (48-50), VII (50-54).

Beccafumi, Domenico (artist): Florence, VII (50-54); Siena, II (136-138).

Bernardi, Giovanni da Castel Bolognese, see Giovanni da Castel Bolognese.

Bertani, Giovan Battista (artist): Mantua, III (72-74).

Bibbiena, il, see Dovizi, Bernardo.

Bonaccorso, Jacopo di, see Jacopo di Bonaccorso.

Bronzino, Agnolo (artist): Florence VII (50-54).

Brusasorzi, il (Domenico del Riccio) (artist): Bologna, III (19-25).

Bugiardini, Giuliano (artist): Florence III (39-43).

Buglioni, Sandro or Santi (artist): Florence, VII (50-54).

Cabeçón, Antonio de (composer and musician): Genoa, IV (61-63).

Caldara, Polidoro, see Polidoro da Caravaggio.

Candia, Giorgio di (author): Pavia, II (106).

Capodiferro, Maddaleni (author): Rome, VI (119-124).

Carota, Antonio di Marco di Giano, called il (artist): Florence, II (38-39).

Carucci, Jacopo, see Pontormo, il.

Cesare (artist): Florence, V (46-48).

Ciatto (artist): Florence, I (35-37).

Cinthio, see Giraldi Cinthio, Giovan Battista.

Conti, Domenico (artist): Florence, VII (50-54).

Corso di Giovanni, see Jacopo di Bonaccorso.

Contile, Luca (author): Milan, IX (91-94).
Corteccia, Francesco (composer): Florence, VII (50-54).

Della Parte, Antonio, see Particini, Antonio.
Domenico del Riccio, see Brusasorzi, il.
Dovizi, Bernardo, called il, or da, Bibbiena (author): Mantua, II (70-72).

Ermanno Fiammingo (artist): Rome, VII (125-129).

Feltrini, Andrea di Cosimo (artist): Florence, II (38-39), III (39-43), IV (43-46), V (46-48), VI (48-50).
Festa, Costanzo (composer): Florence, VII (50-54).
Foschi, Pier Francesco, see Pier Francesco di Sandro.
Fossi, Pietro de' (composer): Venice, II (144-146).
Francesco di Cristoforo, or di Cristofano, see Franciabigio, il.
Francesco Fiorentino, see Maso, Francesco.
Franciabigio, il (Francesco di Cristoforo) (artist): Florence, IV (43-46).
Franco, Battista, see Battista Franco.

Gelli, Giambattista (author): Florence, VII (50-54).
Gherardi, Cristofano (artist): Florence, V (46-48), VI (48-50).
Ghirlandaio, Ridolfo (artist): Florence, III (39-43), IV (43-46), V (46-48), VII (50-54).
Giorgio di Candia, see Candia, Giorgio di.
Giovanni da Castel Bolognese (Giovanni Bernardi) (artist): Rome, VII (125-229).
Giraldi Cinthio, Giovan Battista (author): Ferrara, III (32-34).
Giulio Romano (Giulio Pippi) (artist): Mantua, I (68-70), II (70-72); Milan, VIII (89-91).
Grana, Lorenzo (author): Rome, VI (119-124).
Granacci, Francesco (artist): Florence, III (39-43).

Heemskerck, Maarten van (artist): Rome, VII (125-129).

Indaco, l': see Maso, Francesco.

Jacopo di Bonaccorso (Corso di Giovanni), called il Baia (artist): Florence, III (39-43).

Landi, Antonio (author): Florence ,VII (50-54).
Leonardo da Vinci (artist): Milan, IV (83-85).
Lippi, Filippino (artist): Florence, I (35-37).
Lombardi, Alfonso (artist): Bologna, III (19-25).
Luca di Frosino (artist): Florence, I (35-37).

Machiavelli, Niccolò (author): Florence, IV (43-46).
Martino Tedesco (artist): Rome, VII (125-129).
Masaconi, Giovan Pietro (composer): Florence, VII (50-54).
Maso, Francesco, called l'Indaco (artist): Rome, VII (125-129).
Melighino, Jacomo, or Jacopo (artist): Rome, VII (125-129).
Montelupo, Baccio da, see Baccio da Montelupo.
Montelupo, Raffaello da, see Raffaello da Montelupo.
Montorsoli, Fra Giovan Angelo (artist): Florence, V (46-48).

Nardi, Jacopo (author): Florence, II (38-39).
Nunziata, Antonio del, see Toto del Nunziata.

Palladio, Blosio (author): Rome, VI (119-124).
Parte, Antonio della, see Particini, Antonio.
Particini, Antonio (artist): Florence, V (46-48).
Perino del Vaga (artist): Florence, III (39-43).
Perugino, Pietro (artist): Florence, I (35-37).
Peruzzi, Baldassare (artist): Bologna, II (17-19); Rome, V (117-119), VI (119-124), VII (125-129).
Piccolomini, Alessandro (author): Milan, IX (91-94); Siena, II (136-138).

Pier Francesco di Sandro (artist): Florence, VII (50-54).
Piero da Sesto (artist): Florence, III (39-43).
Piero di Cosimo (artist): Florence, III (39-43).
Piloto, Giovanni, see Pilotto, Girolamo.
Pilotto, Girolamo, called il Piloto (artist): Rome, VII (125-129).
Pimpinella, Vincenzo (author): Rome, VI (129-124).
Plautus, Titus Maccius (author): Ferrara, I (28-30), II (31-32); Rome, II (113-114), VI (119-124).
Polidoro da Caravaggio (artist): Messina, I (76-78).
Pontormo, Jacopo Carucci, called il Pontormo (artist): Florence, II (38-39), III (39-43).
Portelli da Loro, Carlo (artist): Florence, VII (50-54).
Porzio, Camillo (author): Rome, VI (119-124).

Raffaello, see Raphael.
Raffaello da Montelupo (artist): Florence, V (46-48); Rome, VII (125-129).
Raffaello delle Vivuole (artist): Florence, II (38-39).
Rampollini, Matteo (composer): Florence, VII (50-54).
Raphael (Raffaello Sanzio or Santi) (artist): Rome, V (117-119).
Ricchi, Agostino (author): Bologna, III (19-25).
Riccio, Domenico del, see Brusasorzi, il.
Romano, Giulio, see Giulio Romano.
Rosselli, Pietro (artist): Rome, VI (119-124).
Rosso, Giovanni, see Rosso Fiorentino, il.
Rosso Fiorentino, il (Giovanni Rosso) (artist): Florence, III (39-43).
Rustici, Giovan Francesco (artist): Florence, III (39-43).

Salviati, Francesco (artist): Florence, VII (50-54); Rome, VII (125-129).
Sandrino (artist): Rome, VII (125-129).
San Gallo, Antonio da, the Elder (artist): Florence, I (35-37), III (39-43).
San Gallo, Antonio da, the Younger (artist): Rome, VII (125-129).
San Gallo, Aristotele, or Aristotile (real name, Bastiano) da (artist): Florence, III (39-43), IV (43-46), VI (48-50), VII (50-54).
San Gallo, Bastiano da, see San Gallo, Aristotele da.
San Gallo, Battista da (artist): Rome, VII (125-129).
San Gallo, Bernardino da (artist): Florence, III (39-43).
San Gallo, Francesco da (artist): Florence, V (46-48).
San Gallo, Giuliano da (artist): Florence, I (35-37); Rome, VI (119-124).
Sansovino, Jacopo (Jacopo Tatti) (artist): Florence, III (39-43).
Santi, Raffaello, see Raphael.
Sanzio, Raffaello, see Raphael.
Sarto, Andrea del, see Andrea del Sarto.
Secchi, Niccolò (author): Milan, IX (91-94).
Sesto, Piero da, see Piero da Sesto.
Strozzi, Giovambattista, the Elder (author): Florence, VII (50-54).
Strozzi, Lorenzo (author): Florence, IV (43-46).

Tasso, il (Battista di Marco del Tasso) (artist): Florence, V (46-48).
Tatti, Jacopo d'Antonio, see Sansovino, Jacopo.
Terence (Publius Terentius Afer) (author): Ferrara, III (32-34).
Torni, Francesco, see Maso, Francesco.
Toto (Antonio) del Nunziata (artist): Florence, III (39-43).
Tribolo, il (Antonio) (artist): Florence, V (46-48), VI (48-50), VII (50-54).

Ubertini, Francesco, called il Bachiacca (artist): Florence, VII (50-54).

Vaga, Perino del, see Perino del Vaga.
Vasari, Giorgio (artist): Bologna, III (19-25); Florence, III (39-43), V (46-48), VI (48-50).
Veltroni, Stefano (artist): Florence, V (46-48).
Vinci, Leonardo da, see Leonardo da Vinci.
Vittorio Alessandrino (artist): Rome, VII (125-129).
Vivuole, Raffaello delle, see Raffaello delle Vivuole.

TITLES OF PLAYS AND POEMS,
FIRST LINES OF MUSICAL COMPOSITIONS

Adelchi (comedy): Ferrara, III (32-34).
Alessandro (comedy): Milan, IX (91-94).
Altile (tragedy): Ferrara, III (32-34).
Amor costante, L' (comedy): Siena, II (136-138).
Annunciation (sacra rappresentazione): Florence, I (35-37).
Aridosia, L' (comedy): Florence, VI (48-50).
Asinari (comedy): Ferrara, I (28-30).
Bacchidi (comedy): Ferrara, I (28-30).
« *Bacco, Bacco, euoe* » (madrigal): Florence, VII (50-54).

Calandria, La (comedy): Mantua, II (70-72).
Cassaria, La (comedy): Ferrara, II (31-32).
Cassina (comedy): Ferrara, I (28-30).
Cesarea Gonzaga (comedy): Milan, IX (91-94).
« *Chi ne l'ha tolta ohyme* » (madrigal): Florence, VII (50-54).
« *Come lieta si mostra* » (madrigal): Florence, VII (50-54).
Commedia in versi: Florence, IV (43-46).
Comodo, Il (comedy): Florence, VII (50-54).

« *Ecco la fida ancella* » (madrigal): Florence, VII (50-54).
« *Ecco signore il Tebro* » (madrigal): Florence, VII (50-54).
« *Ecco signor Volterra* » (madrigal): Florence, VII (50-54).
Epidicus (comedy): Ferrara, I (28-30).

Falargho (comedy): Florence, IV (43-46).

« *Guardane almo pastore* » (madrigal): Florence, VII (50-54).

« *Hor chi mai canterà* » (madrigal): Florence, VII (50-54).

Inganni, Gli (comedy): Milan, IX (91-94).
« *Ingredere* » (motet): Florence, VII (50-54).
Interesse, L' (comedy): Milan, IX (91-94).

Lena, La (comedy): Ferrara, II (31-32).
« *Lieta per honorarte* » (madrigal): Florence, VII (50-54).

Mandragola, La (comedy): Florence, IV (43-46).
Menaechmi (comedy): Ferrara, II (31-32); Rome, II (113-114).
Miles gloriosus (comedy): Ferrara, I (28-30).

Negromante, Il (comedy): Ferrara, II (31-32).
« *Non men ch'ogni altra* » (madrigal): Florence, VII (50-54).

« *O begli anni del oro* » (madrigal): Florence, VII (50-54).

Pisana, La (comedy): Florence, IV (43-46).
« *Più che mai vaga e bella* » (madrigal): Florence, VII (50-54).
Poenulus (comedy): Rome, VI (119-124).

Ricevuta dell'imperatore alla Cava, La (comedy): Naples, IV (101-104).

« *Sacro e santo hymeneo* » (madrigal): Florence, VII (50-54).

Sette trionfi del secol d'oro, I (poem): Florence, II (38-39).

Tre tiranni, I (comedy): Bologna, III (19-25).

Trionfo dell'età dell'uomo, Il (poem): Florence, II (38-39).

« *Vattene almo riposo* » (madrigal): Florence, VII (50-54).

« *Vien ten'almo riposo* » (madrigal): Florence, VII (50-54).

PRINCIPAL PARTICIPANTS IN THE FESTIVALS, AND SELECTED PERSONAGES AND PERSONIFICATIONS FROM THE *APPARATI* AND DRAMATIC PRESENTATIONS[1]

« *Abigail* »: Venice, I (143-144).

« *Abraham* »: Turin, I (141-142).

« *Agnello, Saint* »: Naples, IV (101-104).

Alciato, Andrea: Pavia, III (107).

« *Alexander the Great* »: Naples, IV (101-104).

Alexander VI, pope: Rome, I (111-112), II (113-114).

Alfonso II, king of Naples: Naples, I (95-96).

« *Ambrose, Saint* »: Bologna, III (19-25); Milan, II (80-81), III (81-83), VII (88-89).

« *Apollo* »: Bologna, III (19-25); Florence, VII (50-54); Rome, V (117-119).

Aragon, Sancha de: Naples, I (95-96).

« *Argos* »: Mantua, III (72-74).

Ariosto, Ludovico: Mantua, II (70-72).

« *Augustus Caesar* »: Bologna, III (19-25); Rome, VII (125-129).

Austria, Caterina d', *duchess of Mantua*: Mantua, IV (74-75).

Austria, Margaret of, see *Margaret of Austria*.

« *Bacchus* »: Bologna, III (19-25).

Barbarini, Agostino, doge of Venice: Venice, I (143-144).

Bordigallo, Dominico: Cremona, I (26-27).

Borgia, Cesare: Rome, II (113-114).

Borgia, Goffre: Naples, I (95-96).

Borgia, Lucrezia: Ferrara, I (28-30); Rome, II (113-114).

Bovio, Giacomo, senator of Rome: Rome, VI (119-124).

Burchard, Johann: Rome, I (111-112).

Calandra, Sabino: Mantua, II (70-72), IV (74-75).

Castiglione, Baldassare: Milan, II (80-81).

« *Cerberus* »: Trent, I (138-140).

« *Charlemagne, emperor* »: Bologna, III (19-25); Siena, I (135-136); Turin, I (141-142).

Charles V, emperor: preface, 6, 7, 8, 10, 11, 15; Bologna, III (19-25); Florence, V (46-48); Genoa, III (60-61); Lucca, II (65-66), III (66-67); Mantua, I (68-70), II (70-72); Messina, I (76-78); Milan, VIII (89-91); Naples, IV (101-104); Rome, VII (125-129); Siena, II (136-138).

Charles VIII, king of France: preface, 7, 8, 10, 13; Florence, I (35-37); Lucca, I (64-65); Naples, II (96-99); Pavia, I (105-106); Pisa, I (108-110); Rome, I (111-112); Siena, I (135-136); Turin, I (141-142).

Cherea, il (Francesco de' Nobili); Florence, IV (43-46).

Chigi, Agostino: Rome, V (117-119).

Christine of Denmark, duchess of Milan: Milan, VII (88-89).

---

[1] Artists, authors of plays and verses, composers, and musicians are indexed separately. The personages and personifications from the *apparati* and dramatic skits are listed in quotation marks.

« Cities, personified »: Florence, VII (50-54); Milan, III (81-83), IV (83-85), VIII (89-91), IX (91-94); Rome, II (113-114), IV (116).

Clement VII, pope: Bologna, III (19-25).

Comines, Philippe: Venice, I (143-144).

« Constantine I, emperor »: Bologna, III (19-25); Rome, VII (125-129).

« Cosmas, Saint »: Rome, V (117-119).

« Cybele », Rome, VI (119-124).

« Damianus, Saint »: Rome, V (117-119).

Danimarca, Cristina di, see Christine of Denmark.

« David »: Milan, IX (91-94); Venice, I (143-144).

Dazzi, Andrea: Florence, II (38-39).

Del Fiesco, Gian Luigi: Genoa, I (56-57).

« Deus Capitolinus »: Rome, VI (119-124).

Donà, Francesco, doge of Venice: Venice, V (148).

Doria, Andrea: preface, 8; Genoa, III (60-61), IV (61-63).

Du Bellay, Cardinal Jean: Rome, IX (130-131).

Duprat, Antoine, chancellor of France: Bologna, II (17-19).

Este, Alfonso I d', duke of Ferrara: Ferrara, I (28-30), II (31-32).

Este, Ercole I d', duke of Ferrara: Ferrara, I (28-30), II (31-32).

Este, Ercole II d', duke of Ferrara: Ferrara, II (31-32), III (32-34).

Este, Cardinal Ippolito d': Rome, II (113-114).

Este, Isabella d', marchioness of Mantua: Ferrara, I (28-30), II (31-32); Mantua, I (68-70); Milan, III (81-83).

« Evangelists »: Rome, VII (125-129).

Farnese, Vittoria, duchess of Urbino: Venice, V (148).

« Fathers, Old Testament »: Rome, VII (125-129).

Ferdinand, king of Aragon and of Naples: preface, 7; Naples, III (99-100); Savona, I (133-134).

Fiesco, see Del Fiesco.

Foix, Anne de, queen of Hungary: Venice, II (144-146).

Foix, Germaine de, queen of Aragon and of Naples: Naples, II (96-99); Savona, I (133-134).

« Fortune »: Milan, V (85-86).

Francis I, king of France: preface, 7; Bologna, II (17-19); Milan, VI (86-88).

Gabrieli, Angelo: Venice, II (144-146).

« Gennaro, San »: Naples, IV (101-104).

« Gervasius, Saint »: Milan, VII (88-89).

« Giants »: Naples, IV (101-104).

« Glory »: Bologna, III (19-25).

Giovio, Paolo: Bologna, II (17-19).

Giustiniani, Stefano: Genoa, II (58-60).

« God the Father »: Bologna, III (19-25).

« Goliath »: Milan, IX (91-94).

Gonzaga, Elisabetta, duchess of Urbino: Ferrara, I (28-30).

Gonzaga, Federico II, marquess, and then duke, of Mantua: Mantua, I (68-70), II (70-72).

Gonzaga, Ferrante: Mantua, IV (74-75); Milan, IX (91-94).

Gonzaga, Francesco II, marquess of Mantua: Milan, II (80-81).

Gonzaga, Francesco III, duke of Mantua: Mantua, III (72-74), IV (74-75).

Gonzaga, Ippolita: Milan, IX (91-94).

Gritti, Andrea, doge of Venice: Venice, III (146).

Guicciardini, Francesco: Florence, V (46-48).

« Habsburg sovereigns »: Bologna, III (19-25); Genoa, IV (61-63); Mantua, I (68-70); Milan, VIII (89-91), IX (91-94); Naples, IV (101-104); Rome, VII (125-129).

« Hannibal »: Messina, I (76-78); Naples, IV (101-104).

« Helen of Troy »: Venice, II (144-146).

Henry II, king of France: preface, 10.

« Hercules »: Florence, III (39-43), V (46-48); Genoa, IV (61-63); Mantua, III (72-74); Trent, I (138-140); Turin, I (141-142).

« Hilaritas publica »: Mantua, III (72-74).

« Humanitas »: Naples, IV (101-104).

« *Indian (Red)* »: Milan, VIII (89-91).
Inghirami, Tommaso: Rome, VI (119-124).
« *Isaac* »: Turin, I (141-142).
« *Iris* »: Mantua, I (68-70).
« *Italy* »: Milan, III (81-83), IX (91-94);
Rome, IV (116); Venice, I (143-144).

« *Jacob* »: Naples, III (99-100).
« *Janus* »: Bologna, III (19-25); Genoa, IV
(61-63); Mantua, III (72-74); Naples,
III (99-100).
« *Januarius, Saint* », see « *Gennaro, San* ».
« *Jason* »: Florence, V (46-48); Turin, I
(141-142).
« *John the Baptist, Saint* »: Rome, V (117-
119).
« *Jove* »: Milan, III (81-83); Naples, IV
(101-104).
Julius II, pope: preface, 9; Bologna, I (15-
17); Rome, III (114-115); IV (116).
Julius III, pope: Rome, X (131-132).
« *Julius Caesar* »: Bologna, III (19-25);
Lucca, I (64-65); Naples, IV (101-104);
Rome, II (113-114); X (131-132).
« *Justice* »: Cremona, I (26-27); Florence,
V (46-48); Genoa, III (60-61); Rome,
VI (119-124); Venice, III (146).

« *Lancelot of the Lake* »: Turin, I (141-142).
*La Tour d'Auvergne, Madeleine de, duchess of
Urbino*: Florence, II (38-39).
Leo X, pope: preface, 7; Bologna, II (17-19);
Florence, II (38-39), III (39-43); Rome,
V (117-119), VI (119-124).
« *Liberty* »: Genoa, IV (61-63).
Loredan, Leonardo, doge of Venice: Venice,
II (144-146).
Louis XII, king of France: preface, 7, 8,
10; Cremona, I (26-27); Genoa, I (56-
57), II (58-60); Milan, II (80-81), III
(81-83), IV (83-85); Pavia, II (106);
Savona, I (133-134).

*Madruzzo, Cardinal Cristoforo di, prince of
Trent*: Trent, I (138-140).
*Margaret of Austria, daughter of Emperor
Charles V and duchess of Florence*: Flor-
ence, VI (48-50); Naples, IV (101-104).

« *Mark, Saint* »: Milan, II (80-81); Venice,
III (146).
« *Mars* »: Milan, III (81-83); Naples, III
(99-100), IV (101-104).
Medici, Alessandro de', duke of Florence, Flor-
ence, V (46-48), VI (48-50).
Medici, Cosimo I de', duke of Florence:
preface, 6, 8; Florence, VII (50-54),
VIII (55).
Medici, Cardinal Giovanni de', see *Leo X*.
« *Medici, Giovanni (Giovanni delle Bande
Nere)* »: Florence, VII (50-54).
Medici, Giuliano de': Florence, II (38-39);
Rome, VI (119-124).
Medici, Lorenzo de', duke of Urbino: Flor-
ence, II (38-39), IV (43-46); Rome, VI
(110-124).
Medici, Ottaviano de': Florence, VI (48-50).
Medici, Pierfrancesco de',: Florence, I (35-37).
« *Mercury* »: Mantua, I (68-70), II (70-72);
Milan, IX (91-94).
« *Minerva* »: Milan, IX (91-94).
« *Moors* »: Messina, I (76-78); Milan, VIII
(89-91).
« *Muses* »; Bologna, III (19-25); Florence,
VII (50-54); Rome, V (117-119).

Nardi, Jacopo: Florence, II (38-39).
« *Neptune* »: Bologna, II (19-25); Trent, I
(138-140).
Nobili, Francesco de', see *Cherea, il*.

« *Ocno* »: Mantua, III (72-74).
« *Orpheus* »: Naples, I (95-96).
« *Orsini, Clarice, mother of Pope Leo X* »:
Rome, VI (119-124).

« *Paris* »: Venice, II (144-146).
« *Paul, Saint* »: Bologna, III (19-25); Rome,
VII (125-129).
Paul III, pope: Ferrara, III (32-34); Lucca,
III (66-67); Rome, VII (125-129), VIII,
(129-130).
« *Peace* »: Cremona, I (26-27); Mantua, I
(68-70); Messina, I (76-78).
Peruzzi, Baldassare: Bologna, II (17-19).
« *Peter, Saint* »: Bologna, III (19-25); Rome,
V (117-119), VII (125-129).

«Petronius, Saint»: Bologna, III (19-25).

Phillip, prince of Spain, son of Emperor Charles V: preface, 7, 8; Cremona, II (27); Genoa, IV (61-63); Mantua, III (72-74); Milan, IX (91-94); Pavia, III (107); Trent, I (138-140).

Pontano, Giovanni: Naples, II (96-99).

Portogallo, Beatrice di, duchess of Savoy: Bologna, III (19-25).

Priuli, Girolamo: Venice, II (144-146).

«Protasius, Saint»: Milan, VII (88-89).

Renée de France, duchess of Ferrara: Ferrara, II (31-32).

Ricci, Pier Francesco: Florence, VIII (55).

«Rivers»: Florence, V (46-48), VII (50-54); Milan, VIII (89-91); Siena, II (136-138); Trent, I (138-140).

San Severino, Cardinal: Rome, II (113-114).

Sanudo, Marino: Venice, II (144-146).

Savoia, Bianca di, duchess of Savoy: Turin, I (141-142).

Scipio Africanus, major and minor: Bologna, III (19-25); Genoa, IV (61-63); Messina, I (76-78); Naples, IV (101-104); Rome, II (113-114).

Sforza, Francesco II, duke of Milan: Milan, VII (88-89); Venice, IV (147).

Sforza, Ludovico il Moro, duke of Milan: Milan, I (79-80).

Sforza, Massimiliano, duke of Milan: Milan, V (85-86).

Sigismundus, emperor: Bologna, III (19-25).

«Tarpeia»: Rome, VI (119-124).

Toledo, Eleonora di, duchess of Florence: Florence, VII (50-54).

Trecco, Ludovico: Cremona, I (26-27).

Trivulzio, Gian Giacomo: Milan, III (81-83).

«Turk»: Milan, VIII (89-91).

Ubaldino, Feriano di: Bologna, II (17-19).

«Vergil»: Cremona, II (27); Mantua, III (72-74).

«Victory»: Bologna, III (19-25); Mantua, I (68-70); Messina, I (76-78); Milan, III (81-83), VIII (89-91).

Vida, Girolamo: Mantua, IV (74-75).

«Virgin Mary»: Milan, VI (86-88); Siena, I (135-136).

«Virtues»: Bologna, III (19-25); Florence, III (39-43), V (46-48); Genoa, IV (61-63); Mantua, III (72-74); Messina, I (76-78); Milan, III (81-83), V (85-86); Naples, IV (101-104); Rome, VI (119-124); Siena, II (136-138).

«War»: Mantua, I (68-70).

Zink, Johannes: Rome, V (117-119).

Zocco, Filippo: Mantua, II (70-72).

AUTHORS OF SOURCES AND STUDIES, SCHOLARLY EDITORS

Celani, Enrico, 150.
Cenci, Pio, 156.
Cerretani, B., 37.
Ceruti, Antonio, 156.
Cessi, Roberto, 157.
Charles VIII, king of France, 97, 98-99, 110, 111.
Chartrou, Josèphe, 37, 83, 84, 85, 142, 151.
Chastel, André, 48, 69, 127, 138, 151.
Cherrier, C. de, 37, 65, 98, 106, 110, 112, 136, 142, 151.
Chiappelli, Fredi, 45.
Chierigato, Francesco, 41, 121.
Cimber, M. L. (real name Lafaist), 36, 58, 98, 105, 109, 112, 135, 141, 151, 152, 155.
Civitali, Giuseppe, 66.
Clementi, Filippo, 114, 116, 131, 132, 151.
Coleine, Cola, 131.
Comines, Philippe de, 109, 143, 144, 151.
Commynes, see Comines.
Coniglio, Giuseppe, 69.
Constant, G., 23.
Contarini del Zaffo, Alvise Carlo, 147.
Conti da Foligno, Sigismondo de', 16.
Coppi, Anna Maria, 29.
Corazzini, Giuseppe Odoardo, 155, 155-156.
Creighton, Mandell, 121, 151.
Creizenach, Wilhelm, 29, 93, 151.
Cruciani, Fabrizio, 117, 119, 121, 122, 123, 124.

D'Alibrando, see Alibrando.
D'Ancona, Alessandro, 29, 31, 49, 53, 71, 74, 83, 114, 123, 140, 142, 144, 151.
Danjou, F., 151.
Danza, Paolo, 102, 129-130.
D'Arco, Carlo, 29.
De Angelis D'Ossat, Guglielmo, 126, 127, 129.
Delaborde, H.-François, 37, 65, 98, 106, 110, 112, 136, 142, 151.
Del Badia, Iodoco, 154.
Delicati, Pio, 154.
Dell'Arco, M. Fagiolo, 5.
De Simone, Cornelio, 59.
Desjardins, Abel, 59, 151-152.

Desrey, Pierre, 36, 64, 105, 109, 135, 141, 142, 152.
Díaz, Vasco, 25.
Dina, Achille, 79.
Dorez, Léon, 127.
Durville, G., 151.

Egger, Hermann, 117, 119, 126, 127, 128, 129, 152.
Equicola D'Alveto, Mario, 152.
Este, Isabella d', marchioness of Mantua, 29, 30, 70, 83.
Estissac, Bishop Geoffroy d', 126.

Fabbri, Mario, 45, 50, 53, 152.
Fabbri, Paolo, 73, 74, 75, 152.
Fabroni, Angelo, 152, and in the Addenda.
Faccioli, Emilio, 50, 70, 71, 74, 75, 152.
Farnese Della Rovere, Vittoria, 148.
Faustini, Dottore, 34, 158.
Ferriero di Lauriano, Francesco Maria, 142.
Filangieri, Riccardo, 100.
Fiorani, L., 115, 119, 128, 152.
Fiorini, Vittorio, 156.
Firmani, Giovan Francesco, 33.
Fleuranges, see Florange.
Florange, Seigneur de (Robert de la Marck), 18, 84, 85, 87, 152.
Foglietta, Umberto, 56, 59, 152.
Fontana, Bartolommeo, 32, 33, 152.
Forcella, Vincenzo, 126, 128, 130, 131, 152-153.
Frati, Luigi, 154.
Frizzi, Antonio, 30, 32, 33, 153.
Frommel, Christoph Luitpold, 17, 18, 117, 119, 153, and in the Addenda.
Fulin, Rinaldo, 158.
Fuscolillo, Gaspare, 99.

Gabbioneta, Alessandro, 19.
Gabotto, Ferdinando, 142.
Gabrieli, Angelo, 145.
Gachard, Louis Prosper, 77, 102, 153, 156, 159.
Gaddi, Angelo and Francesco, 36.
Gaeta Bertalà, Giovanna, 5.
Garbero Zorzi, Elvira, 152.
Garzilli, Paolo, 153.
Gelli, Agenore, 156.

Saint Gelais, Octavien de, 155.
Sala, Andrea, 47, 77, 78, 103, 104, 126, 127, 128, 137, 158.
Salimbene, Antonio, 144.
Salvago, Alessandro, 59.
Sanesi, Ireneo, 25, 32, 46, 50, 54, 94, 101, 104, 158.
San Luigi, Fra Ildefonso di, 150-151.
Santa Cruz, Alonso de, 22, 23, 27, 47, 61, 63, 66, 67, 69, 71, 73, 77, 90, 92, 93, 100, 103, 107, 127, 130, 134, 137, 140, 158.
Sanudo, Marino, 16, 18, 22, 23, 29, 37, 42, 44, 57, 59, 64, 69, 79, 81, 83, 85, 86, 88, 98, 100, 106, 109, 112, 114, 115, 118, 122, 135, 141, 144, 145, 146, 147, 158.
Sardi, Gasparo, 29, 31, 34, 158.
Saxl, F., 94.
Schaeffer, Emil, 43.
Scheurl, Christoph, in the Addenda.
Schmarsow, R., 15, 149.
Secchi, Niccolò, 93.
Segre, Arturo, 80, 157.
Senarega, Bartolommeo, 57, 59, 158.
Serassi, Abbate Pier Antonio, 80.
Serdonati, Francesco, 152.
Sereno, Aurelio, 121, 122, 123, 124.
Settimanni, Francesco, 49, 53.
Sforza, Francesco II, duke of Milan, 147.
Shearman, John, 38, 39, 40, 41, 42, 43.
Siculo, Giulio Simone, 122.
Simonetti, Adolfo, 67.
Singleton, Charles, 38, 39.
Solerti, Angelo, 54.
Sorbelli, Albano, 16.
Stabellini, Battista, 116.
Stefani, Federico, 88.
Stirling, Sir William, *see* Maxwell.
Strong, Anthony, 25, 48, 77, 78, 91, 104, 129, 138, 158.

Summonte, Giovan Antonio, 96, 99, 100, 101, 104, 158.

Tamassia Mazzarotta, Bianca, 146.
Tedallini, Sebastiano di Branca, 112, 114, 115, 118, 122, 158.
Terlinden, Vicomte, 25.
Testa, Francesco, 145.
Thuasne, Louis, 150.
Toca, Mircea, 126, 129.
Tommaso, Antonio G., 78.
Tommaso de Catania, 103.
Tosi, C. O., 55.
Treccani degli Alfieri, Conte Giovanni, 81, 83, 86, 88, 89, 91, 94, 158.
Trotta (Ferrarese ambassador), 94.
Truffi, Riccardo, 158.
Tuttavilla, Girolamo, 98.

Ulloa, Alfonso, 27, 63, 73, 74, 93, 140, 159.

Vaissière, Pierre de, 150.
Valbusa, D., 150.
Vandenesse, Jean de, 12, 22, 47, 61, 66, 67, 69, 71, 90, 103, 127, 137, 159.
Varchi, Benedetto, 47, 49, 61, 159.
Vasari, Giorgio, 22, 39, 42, 44, 47-48, 49, 52, 69, 71, 77, 103, 122, 127, 137, 138, 159.
Vellutello, Alessandro, 22.
Vianello, C., 94.
Vigo, Pietro, 137.
Vizani, Pompeo, 17, 19, 25, 159.
Volpi, Giuseppe, 65, 66.

Zambotti, Bernardino, 28, 29, 114, 159.
Zenatti, Albino, 140.
Zippel, Giuseppe, 150.
Zorzi, Ludovico, 30, 50, 51, 54, 124, 152, 159.
Zorzi, Marino, 42.

TABLE OF CONTENTS